Indoor Hockey

BK4311

Sports

C000024778

Indoor

Sue Slocombe and Carl Ward

This book is due for return on or before the last date shown below.

A & C Black · London

First published 1985
by A & C Black (Publishers) Limited
35 Bedford Row, London, WC1R 4JH

Slocombe, Sue
    Indoor hockey.
    1. Indoor hockey
    I. Title   II. Ward, Carl
    796.35'5   GV1017.I/

    ISBN 0-7136-2463-9

Printed in Great Britain by A. Wheaton Co & Ltd, Exeter.

Acknowledgements
The authors are indebted to the following for their contributions: Angela Wright,
David Ward and Tom Ward (and all the players who appear in the book) for
demonstrations; Rob Wyatt, Claire Haynes and Alberto Troiano for photography;
and Denise Griffiths, John Cadman and Melvyn Pignon for advice.

Contents

Introduction

If you've ever played outdoor hockey, you'll realise when you have a go at the indoor game how beneficial it is – hockey sharpens footwork, stickwork, anticipation and general fitness. If you've never even played outdoor hockey, then the indoor game is a wonderful start – a compact, enjoyable game which develops an agile manipulation of both physical and mental abilities.

Indoor hockey is a fun team game which can be played and enjoyed from a young age. The basic skills can then be mastered early through active involvement in games like 'Crazy Hockey', Roller Ball, Consecutive Hockey and other small sided games which are discussed further in Chapter 6 (see page 44). The game need not be limited to those possessing indoor sticks, indoor balls and easy access to a sports hall, as use can be made of any suitable and available equipment, including shinty sticks, unihoc sticks, airflow balls, and similar equipment often found in primary and secondary schools.

We would like primary aged children to experience a fun and exciting invasion (team) game utilising available equipment, but as the young players become more proficient then the correct equipment should be employed to help them develop their skills and tactics further.

Indoor hockey is a fluid game in which players are constantly changing roles. It is built around the basic skills of passing and receiving to build up attacks, and is similar to basketball in that when a team has possession each of its players attacks, and when the opposition has possession, each defends. Success is achieved by high levels of individual skill and co-ordinated play.

The main features of indoor hockey are:

1. The formation of a squad, with a maximum of twelve players. Six players take the court at any one time, usually a goalkeeper and five court players.
2. The use of substitution as a tactical ploy; this is discussed further in Chapter 10 (see page 91).
3. The use of the push or slap pass. The hit or drive is not permitted.
4. The ball may only be lifted when making a shot at goal.
5. The ball must not be played in the air.
6. The ball may be played off the side-boards.
7. There is no offside.
8. Long corners are never awarded.

Equipment and facilities

Ideally indoor hockey is played in a sports hall, but a gymnasium, hall, netball court, playground or hard hockey pitch can be adapted to accommodate the game. Forms can be turned upside down so that the small lip is used to play off; gymnastic planks, or wood measuring approximately 10 cm square and 2 to 4 metres long can be laid down end to end to create side-boards.

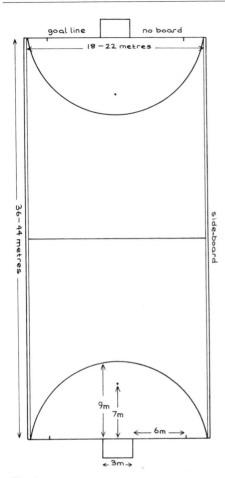

Fig. 1
Plan of pitch in metres.

Fig. 2
A cross section showing the dimensions of the side-boards.

Goals

Initially skittles, cones, bibs and benches can be used. In a gym, two goals 3 metres wide and 2 metres high can be marked with tape on the walls. Eventually it is advisable to purchase goals that are mobile and can easily be stored when not in use.

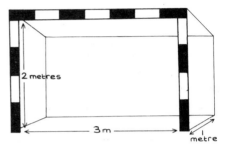

Fig. 3
Dimensions of an indoor goal.

The stick

There are specially designed sticks and balls for indoor hockey and it is vital to employ the correct equipment if players are to develop the right skills. However, when initiating the game, the teacher or coach may adapt the equipment already available in the school or club. It is a pity that many schools shy away from the game due to a lack of the correct equipment, since unihoc sticks, shinty sticks, polypropolene sticks and field hockey sticks can be used in the early stages. If introducing indoor hockey on a playground or tennis court, then it is useful to tape the head of the sticks to minimise wear.

The indoor stick is lighter than an outdoor stick, with a specially designed head which makes stopping, tackling and ball control, in general, easier. It is essential to develop good playing skills with the correct

5

length stick; there is a wide range of sticks available, from 21 inches to 38 inches.

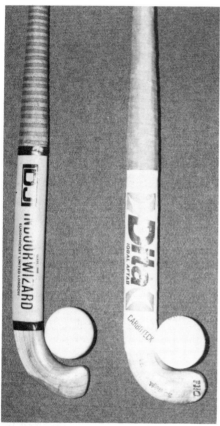

Note the specially designed head of the indoor hockey stick on the left.

The ball

An indoor hockey ball can be white or coloured, usually yellow or orange, weighs between 156 and 163 grammes, and has a circumference of between 22·4 cm and 23·5 cm. It is lighter than a field hockey ball.

When introducing the game to young players mini-hockey balls weighing 3½ oz may be used making it easier to put pace on the ball. However, the teacher or coach may decide to use a larger or lighter ball.

Grids

Players can be organised more easily into particular practices and games by using grids which are squares or rectangles marked on the playing surface. More often, markings already laid for other games like tennis, badminton and netball can be utilised, or cones, bibs, skittles or other similar equipment placed as markers.

Many of the practices in the following chapters have been organised using one or more grids to assist the coach in quick and simple organisation.

Key	
path of player without ball	$- - - - \rightarrow$
path of player with ball	$\sim\sim\sim\rightarrow$
path of ball	$\longrightarrow$
shot at goal	$\Longrightarrow$

1

Basic skills – passing and receiving

The two techniques which are most used in indoor hockey are those of passing and receiving, and in order for individuals to achieve success, they must be able to give accurate passes, and receive passes, both in a stationary position and on the move.

In the early stages a great deal of time should be spent developing these two elementary skills.

Passing techniques

The ball must not be hit, nor must it be lifted except when making a shot at goal. The only way to pass is to push, slap or deflect it. To make it easier for the receiver, the passer should aim to pass to the receiver's open stick-side, just outside the right foot.

A THE PUSH PASS

This is the most common way of passing, and is most effective and accurate over short distances.

The grip: Hands should be held comfortably apart on the stick with the left hand at the top. The right hand should be approximately half-way down the shaft – lowering the right hand helps to give greater control. Both hands should grasp the stick firmly.

Body position: The body should be crouched with the knees bent and facing sideways, with the left foot pointing in the direction the ball is to travel. The feet should be ½ to 1 metre apart, and the head over or in line with the ball.

Push pass: *Stage 1* Note the stick in contact with the ball.

Stage 2 Note how the body weight has been transferred from the right foot to the left foot.

The stick and ball: The stick begins a short distance behind the ball *on the ground*, with the stick face angled towards the ground.

The slap: *Stage 1* Note the distance of the stick from the ball.

Stage 3 Note the follow-through of stick and body weight.

The stick and ball: The stick should be held away from the body, with the stick head in contact with the ground and the ball, and angled towards the ground to prevent the ball bouncing upwards. Position the ball between the feet.

Making the pass: In making the pass the stick must be in contact with the ball from the beginning of the movement to the point of release. Transfer the body weight from the right foot to the left foot, propelling the ball forwards, and follow through in the direction the ball is to travel.

Stage 2 Note the angle of the stick.

B THE SLAP

This is used almost as often as the push pass. The techniques involved are similar, but while the push pass is most effective over short distances, the slap is used to make long, powerful, penetrative passes.

The grip and body position: As for the push pass.

Stage 3 Note the follow-through of the stick and body weight.

Making the pass: The stick is brought into contact with the ball with a 'sweeping' action, keeping the stick constantly in contact with the ground, and angled towards the ground to ensure the ball is not lifted. Follow through in the direction the ball is to travel. To make a more powerful pass, increase the distance and speed of the sweep and use the body weight more, stepping from the right to the left foot while executing the shot.

C THE DEFLECTED PASS – WALL PASS – ONE/TWO COMBINATION

This is the most difficult pass to make and requires a certain level of proficiency before it can be practised successfully. It is more effective over short distances of 1 to 5 metres, and is particularly useful at free pass situations when using a tightly marked player to give a return pass or deflection. It can also be used when two attackers are attempting to beat a defender and need to exchange short, quick passes when there is little time and space. The player making this pass does not stop the ball but redirects it with a first time touch (see fig. 4).

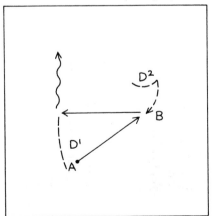

Fig. 4 The wall pass.

The player with the ball:
1. Should always commit the defending player, unless it is a free pass situation.
2. Should pass to the open-stick side of the player acting as the wall.
3. On releasing the ball should accelerate into the space behind the defender in order to receive the return pass.

The player acting as the wall:
The grip: As for the push pass.
Body position: The body should be crouched and the knees bent. The player should stand sideways with the left shoulder pointing in the direction from which the ball is coming.
The stick and ball: The stick should be held almost horizontal and as low as possible, with the face angled towards the ground so that the ball is not lifted when making the return pass.

This pass can also be played with an upright stick by more advanced players; it is similar to a forward defensive stroke in cricket.

Making the pass: The player will not have possession of the ball – it will be passed to him/her from another direction. When the ball arrives, the player should move the stick, held low, along the ground towards the ball, and gently push or deflect it in the chosen direction without stopping it. The pass should be the same as if the sideboards had been used to deflect the ball.

Receiving techniques

No matter how good players are at passing a ball, they will be of little use to the team if their control when receiving a pass is poor. In a game, a player will be expected to receive passes in two situations.

1. In *space*, with plenty of time before he/she is put under pressure.
2. Under *pressure* with little time during which he/she must create space.

A RECEIVING IN SPACE

On receiving a pass in space the player should 'kill' the ball or attempt to stop it dead. This allows the player more time to look up and assess the situation before *passing*, *dribbling* or *shooting*.

Receiving on the open-stick side

The grip: As for the push pass.

Body position: Crouched sideways, in a low position, with feet apart and knees bent.

The stick: Should be almost horizontal to the ground, and angled towards the ground to trap the ball. On receiving the ball immediately move the feet into a position to *pass*, *dribble* or *shoot*.

Receiving on the open-stick side.

Receiving on the reverse-stick side

The grip: The stick can be held in both hands to give greater strength but it is usual for the left hand only to be used as it allows a more balanced position and makes it possible to receive a pass wide of the body.

Body position: A low body position should be adopted with knees bent. The receiver should step forward onto the left foot to receive the ball out in front of the body.

The stick: After turning the stick over into a reverse-stick position place the stick in front of the left foot with the 'toe' of the stick and knuckles of the left hand in contact with the ground. Angle the stick towards the body so that if the ball is not stopped cleanly at the first attempt it will be deflected towards you and not away, thereby giving you a second chance to regain control.

Receiving a pass at the feet

This method of receiving is not used as frequently as the other two but sometimes it is necessary to receive a ball close to the feet.

The grip: The stick is held in two hands, although sometimes the right hand only is used as it allows a more balanced position.

Body position: Once again, a low body position should be adopted with knees bent and the player facing the incoming ball. Step forwards slightly onto the left foot.

The stick: Turn the stick over and make sure the 'toe' and knuckle of the right hand are in contact with the ground. Angle the stick towards the ground. On receiving in this way, immediately turn the stick to the usual position to gain control of the ball ready to *pass*, *dribble* or *shoot*.

Receiving on the reverse-stick side.

The player in the dark strip prepares to receive a pass under pressure on the open-stick side.

Receiving a pass at the feet. Note the position of the hands, feet and stick.

The player in the dark strip prepares to receive a pass under pressure on the reverse-stick side.

B   RECEIVING A PASS UNDER PRESSURE

Before teachers or coaches introduce this skill, they must be sure that the players are technically proficient at passing a ball to a moving target and receiving a pass on the move. This skill is usually performed with an *upright stick* on both the open and reverse stick sides. This is done so that the ball can be brought under effective control as quickly as possible with the first touch, so allowing the player more time to perform the next move. It is an essential attacking skill and is indispensable when playing at more advanced levels.

Receiving on the open-stick side with an upright stick

The grip: As for the push pass but with the right hand about a third of the way down the shaft of the stick.

Body position: The body should be as near to upright as possible. This is important if the player has to receive the ball on the move in order to create more time and space in which to play the ball.

The stick: The head of the stick should be on the ground near the right foot and angled towards the ground. On impact the ball should be met with a firm, not rigid, stick.

Receiving on the reverse-stick side with an upright stick

The grip: As for the push pass, with the wrists rolled anti-clockwise to turn the stick onto the reverse side.

11

Body position: As with receiving on the open-stick side except that the ball will be received outside the left foot.

The stick: Should be held in the reverse-stick position with the toe of the stick in contact with the ground and inclined towards it. The stick should be held out in front of the body (see photograph) to give greater control.

After receiving on the reverse-stick immediately drag the ball across to the open-stick side ready to *pass, dribble,* or *shoot.*

Practices to develop passing and receiving techniques

1. Each player works on his/her own passing the ball against the wall, side boards or benches from a distance of about 1½ to 3 metres. The push pass, slap pass and first-time pass can be used. The rebound can be received on the open and reverse stick sides using a horizontal and upright stick. The player should remain stationary.

2. Working in pairs with one ball. The players should position themselves about 3 to 5 metres apart and pass the ball to each other using:
    - the push pass
    - the slap pass
    - the deflected pass or wall pass
They should receive the ball on the open and reverse stick sides, using the horizontal and upright stick as required.

3. Four players and one ball to a grid (see fig. 5). The players should position themselves in the four corners of the grid and pass the ball to each other. The ball should be passed clockwise and then anti-clockwise around the

grid using:
    - the push pass
    - the slap pass
The ball should be received on the open and reverse-stick sides, using the horizontal and upright stick techniques as required.

4. Four players and two balls to a grid. Players **A** and **C** start with the balls which are passed around the grid clockwise and then anti-clockwise with the passing and receiving techniques described in exercise 3. The aim of the exercise is to make one ball catch up with the other.
This exercise can also be performed with 6 or 8 players.

5. Three players and one ball to a grid (see fig. 6). Player **A** passes the ball to Player **B** and runs to the free corner in

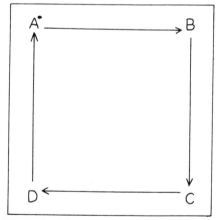

Fig. 5 A - player with ball.
B - 'wall' player. D - defending player.

the grid. Then player **B** passes to player **C** and runs to the free corner, and so on, using:
a the push pass
b the slap pass
c the wall pass

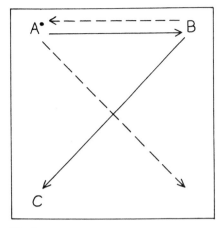

Fig. 6

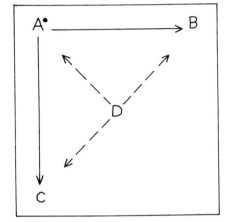

Fig. 6A

When the players have become reasonably proficient at each of these practices the coach can introduce an element of pressure. This can be done by asking the players to make a certain number of passes in a limited time of 30 seconds, 45 seconds or 1 minute.

The practices can be made more difficult by bringing in an opponent who provides either passive or active opposition.

6. Four players and one ball to a grid. Players **A, B** and **C** must pass the ball to each other in the grid and try to make as many passes as they can in 30 seconds. Player **D** must try to intercept the ball and knock it out of the grid to score. The coach can restrict the players to making one type of pass, or players may be allowed to use any of the three techniques described earlier depending on the circumstances in which they find themselves (see fig. 6A).

Practices can also be made more difficult by getting players to pass and receive on the move.

7. Each player has a ball and should run, in turn, towards the cones, skittles or bibs placed around the pitch, pass the ball against the side-boards or wall and pick up the rebound on the other side of the obstacle. N.B. The more acute the angle of the pass the farther the player will have to run to collect the ball off the wall or side-boards. The pass should be made with the open stick and collected with the reverse stick in the upright position (see fig.7).

8. Two players with one ball in a grid. Player **A** passes the ball to player **B** and moves across the grid to position **A**[1]. **B** then passes the ball to **A**[1] and moves across to **B**[1]. **A**[1] passes the ball to **B**[1] and returns to position **A** . The exercise is repeated with players moving across the diagonals and the ball going round the square clockwise. The exercise can be repeated with the ball travelling around the square anticlockwise (see fig. 8).

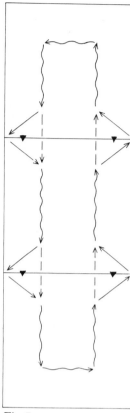

Fig. 7

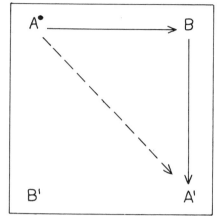

Fig. 8

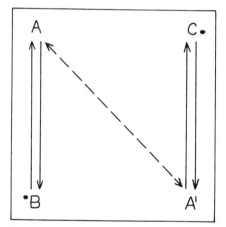

Fig. 9

9. Three players and two balls in a grid. Players **B** and **C** have a ball each. **B** passes to **A** who receives and passes back to **B** before running to position **A**^{1}. At **A**^{1} player **A** receives a pass from **C** and passes back to **C** before returning to position **A**. The exercise can be repeated with player **A** receiving passes on the open- and reverse-stick sides (see fig. 9).

10. Two players and one ball in a grid. Player **A** begins with the ball, runs with it across the grid and passes to

player **B** at the half-way point. **B** receives the ball and repeats the exercise, passing to **A** at **A**^{1} and moving on to **B**^{1}. The exercise can be repeated with the ball being passed with, and received on, the reverse-stick side (see fig. 10).

11. Three players, two balls and two grids. Players **A** and **B** have a ball each and are positioned 10 - 15 metres apart.

14

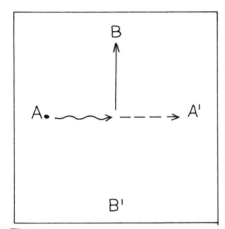

Fig. 10

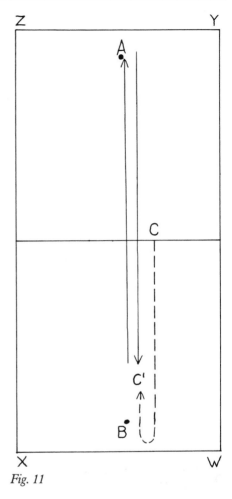

Fig. 11

Player **C** starts in the middle, runs to line **WX** touches it and returns. Player **A** immediately passes to **C** who receives and passes back to **A**. **C** continues running to line **YZ,** touches it and turns to receive a pass from **B**. The pass is returned to **B** and the exercise is repeated for 30 seconds, 45 seconds or 1 minute. The exercise can be performed with the player in the middle receiving passes on the open- and reverse-stick sides. Horizontal and upright stick techniques may also be used when necessary. (See fig. 11)

12. Four players and one ball in a grid. **A** and **B** line up on one side of the grid and **C** and **D** line up on the other. **A** passes to **C** and runs to join the queue behind **D**. **C** receives and immediately passes to **B** and runs on to join the opposite queue. **B** passes to **D, D** to **C, C** to **A,** and so on, for 30 seconds, 45 seconds or 1 minute. 6 or 8 players can be used in one grid if need be. (See fig. 12)

13. Four players and two balls in one grid. **A** and **B** start with the balls; **D** is the target man. **A** passes to **D. D** passes the ball to the player without the ball, **C. B** then passes to **D** who in turn passes to **A** and so on for a given time. Passes can be received on the open- and reverse-stick sides. Both upright and horizontal stick techniques can be used. (See fig. 13)

15

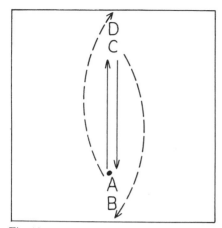

Fig. 12

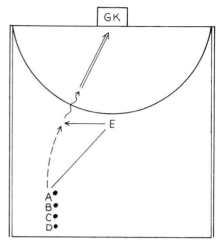

Fig. 14

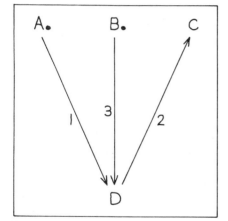

Fig. 13

14. In groups of 5 or 6, each player with a ball. One player from the group positions himself/herself at the top of the circle. The other players in turn pass the ball to this player who deflects the ball with a wall pass or one/two combination into their path. They pick up the pass run into the circle and shoot. Goalkeepers can also be used in this exercise. (See fig. 14)

15. Players **A, B, C,** and **D** are positioned on either side of the pitch. The rest of the group line up at one end of the pitch, each with a ball. In turn players pass to and receive a pass from players **A, B, C,** and **D**. After the final pass they should enter the circle and shoot. Goalkeepers can be used in this exercise. (See fig. 15)

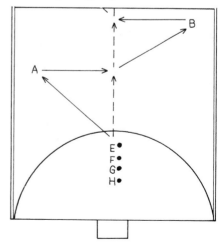

Fig. 15 Beginning of the practice.

2

Basic skills – tackling

All players will find it necessary to challenge an opponent for the ball at some point in the game; therefore all players, but particularly those who play in defensive positions, should learn to tackle effectively on both sides. Above all else a tackler must learn to time the tackle correctly and avoid the temptation to 'rush in' to the tackle. The defender must watch the ball and react to this, not the body movement of the player in possession of the ball. Unlike the outdoor game, players are not allowed to swing or 'throw' their sticks at the ball when making a tackle. Nor is the jab tackle truly effective in indoor hockey, as it tends to cause the ball to lift. *The defender's stick must be in contact with the ground prior to making a tackle.*

Tackling on the open-stick side.

A TACKLING ON THE OPEN-STICK SIDE

The grip: Should be as for the push pass, with the left hand at the top of the stick and the right hand a third to half-way down to give power and support to the tackle.

Body position: As when receiving the ball, the body should be crouched, knees bent and feet apart with the left foot forwards in a well balanced position and the weight on the balls of the feet (see photograph). By turning slightly sideways the defender can force the attacker to move towards their open-stick side, thus making it easier to tackle.

The stick: The tackler should attempt to get the entire length of the stick onto the floor in front of the ball, in a similar way to receiving (see page 11), with the knuckles touching the floor and so offering the maximum stick surface to stop the ball.

Making the tackle: As the attacker attempts to beat the defender on the open-stick side, the defender moves the stick in two hands along the ground to block the pathway of the ball. The stick should be laid in front of the right foot. If the attacker moves wide of the defender, the tackler may need to tackle with one hand on the stick.

If the attacker has gone round the defender, it may be necessary to tackle with the right hand only at the top of the stick, laying the stick behind the line of the right foot (see page 11).

B   TACKLING ON THE
REVERSE-STICK SIDE

It is possible to make a two-handed tackle on the reverse-stick side, but usually circumstances dictate that the reverse-stick tackle is made with only the left hand holding the stick.

The grip: Hold the stick at the top in the left hand only.

Body position: Step forward so that the body weight is on the left foot.

The stick: Lay the stick diagonally in front of the left foot, with the left knee and upper leg almost supporting the arm as the tackle is made (see photograph).

If the attacker takes the ball wide of the defender on this side, the tackle will have to be made outside the line of the left foot. This is rarely a strong or effective tackle.

Tackling on the reverse-stick side.

Suggested stages in teaching tackling

Two players and one ball

1. **A** rolls the ball to **B** about 3 – 5 metres apart; **B** receives on the open-stick/reverse-stick side.
2. **A** dribbles the ball towards **B** to pass on the open-stick/reverse-stick side. **B** tackles, gains possession and accelerates away from **A**.

Initially **A** allows **B** to tackle. As the tackler becomes more proficient **A** should aim to keep possession while **B**, the tackler, becomes determined to gain possession.

Practices to develop tackling

1. Two players and one ball in a grid. **A**, with ball, aims to dribble past or dodge **B** and to stop the ball on line **WZ**, while **B** tries to tackle, gain

A reverse-stick tackle being made during a game. Note the position of the stick and the body weight over the left leg, which in turn supports the arm involved in the tackle.

possession and pass the ball over line **XY**. (See fig. 16)

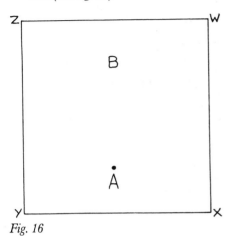

Fig. 16

2. 2 v 1

Three players and one ball in two grids.

A[1], with ball, aims to dribble or dodge past **B** and to stop the ball on line **WZ** to score. **B**[1] aims to tackle **A**[1] before line **XY**, gain possession and pass to **B**[2] to score. (See fig. 17)

3. Small-sided games like 2 v 1, 3 v 1, 3 v 2, give plenty of opportunities for tackling. *For example*, 2 v 1:

A[1] and **A**[2] begin with the ball. They aim to dribble the ball over line **WZ** to score while **D** attempts to intercept or tackle to gain possession and pass the ball over line **XY**. (See fig. 18)

4. 3 v 2

As in 3 but **A**[1] and **A**[2] score by passing to **A**[3] while **D**[1] scores by intercepting the ball and passing to **D**[2]. **A**[3] and **D**[2] must remain on their lines, although they can move along them. (See fig. 19)

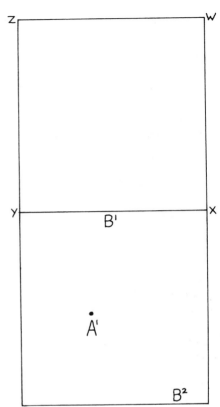

Fig. 17

5. 1 v 1

A[1] aims to dribble past and dodge **D** and shoot. **D** aims to tackle and clear the ball over the half-way line. (See fig. 20)

6. 3 v 2

A[1], **A**[2], and **A**[3] work to get the ball into the circle, and to shoot and score. **GK** and **D** aim to gain possession and clear the ball over the half-way line. (See fig. 21)

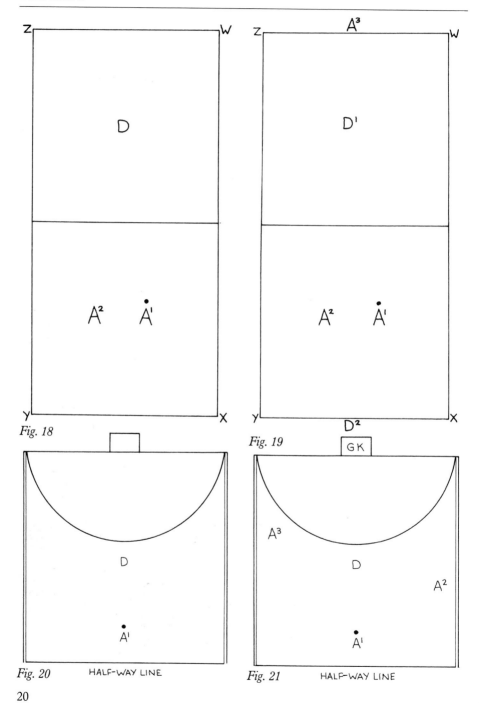

Fig. 18

Fig. 19

Fig. 20   HALF-WAY LINE

Fig. 21   HALF-WAY LINE

3

Basic skills – dribbling, beating an opponent and running with the ball

Dribbling

Most teams contain players who can beat opponents by dribbling or dodging. These players have the ability to create the 'extra player' for their team in attacking situations as well as having the skill to get themselves and their team out of difficult and dangerous defensive situations.

All dribbling and dodging involves risk, the risk of being dispossessed, and teachers and coaches must remember that even the best dribblers in the team are likely to have more failures than successes. Developing the right attitude to the chances of success and failure when dribbling is a very important part of developing this skill. Rather than discouraging players from dribbling, teachers and coaches should make players aware of the importance of the skill and the conditions under which it should be performed:

1. *The stage and state of the game* – dribbling when one's own team is winning comfortably can be relatively safe. Doing so when the scores are equal can be rather risky.
2. *The area of the court involved* – dribbling near or in the opponents' circle can be effective and rewarding, while dribbling near or in one's own circle can prove disastrous.

The ability to dribble, dodge and beat an opponent is based on four qualities:

1. The ability to maintain close control of the ball
2. The ability to feint and 'dummy'
3. The ability to change direction
4. The ability to change pace

The grip

For ease of control the stick should be held with the left hand at the top and the right hand a third to half-way down the shaft.

The 'V' formed by the forefinger and thumb of each hand should run down the spine of the stick (see photograph). Latitude should be allowed for individual preference and comfort.

This shows the grip and the 'V' formed by the forefinger and thumb of each hand.

The rotational movement of the stick is controlled by the left hand while the right hand gives added support and control as the stick is rotated through it. Some players prefer to extend the right finger along the stick as a further aid to control. Both hands must feel comfortable when the stick is held in the open and reverse stick positions.

The body and feet
The body should be held in a crouched but balanced position, with the feet evenly spaced and ready to change pace and direction when necessary. Good, balanced footwork is essential for dribbling.

The stick and ball
The stick and ball should be kept out in front and slightly to the right of the body. From this position the ball can be moved from side to side or forwards and backwards using the open and reverse stick.

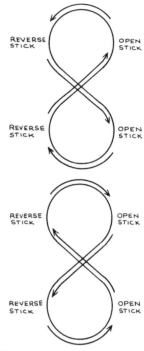

Fig. 22

Practices to develop dribbling skills

At first practices which require the players to move the ball from side to side and forwards and backwards should be done standing still. Once they are confident they should perform the practices at walking pace and then while running.

Examples

1. Each player with a ball should stand with feet slightly apart in a well balanced position. Starting with the ball just outside the right foot they move it across to just outside the left foot and back again using the open and reverse stick.

2. As above but players should move the ball in a figure of eight (see fig. 22).

3. Each player with a ball is required to dribble it around the perimeter of the court, hall or gymnasium while moving forwards, sideways and backwards (see fig. 23).

4. Each player with a ball is allowed to dribble anywhere on the court. They must keep control of the ball and avoid colliding with other players.

5. (See fig. 24) Players form pairs, with one ball to a pair. Number **1** from each couple is positioned somewhere on the court, while number **2** dribbles the ball in and out of the stationary players. After 15-30 seconds they

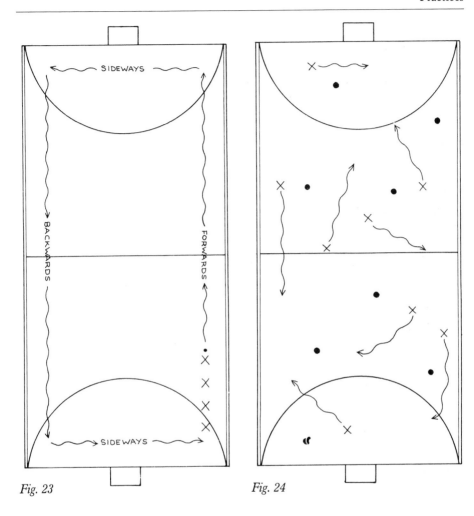

Fig. 23

Fig. 24

should change over so that number **2** stands still while number **1** dribbles around.

6. As for 6, but this time the stationary players are allowed to try to dispossess the players who are dribbling. The stationary players must keep their feet together and are not allowed to move them even when attempting to tackle. The players on the ball must try to

keep possession for 15-30 seconds, at the end of which they change roles.

As the players become more proficient at dribbling and dodging, the area in which they operate can be reduced to make the practice more difficult and so improve their concentration and skill levels.

7. (See fig. 25) Four players and one ball in each grid. Each player in turn dribbles the ball in and out of the obstacles (slalom fashion) and returns to the start to hand over to the next player. Players can be asked to work flat out by turning the practice into a race.

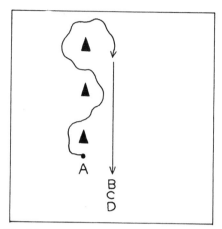

Fig. 26

1. Beating an opponent on the reverse-stick side

The player with the ball should move towards the opponent's open-stick side and as the latter is committed to that side the player with the ball should step off the left foot to the right, pulling the ball with the reverse stick to the open-stick side. The attacker should now accelerate past the opponent's reverse-stick side making it difficult for them to tackle back.

It is important to emphasize the sudden change in direction and pace when performing this move.

2. Beating an opponent on the open-stick side

The player with the ball should move towards the opponent's reverse-stick side. As the opponent is committed to this side the attacker should step off the right foot to the left and drag the ball that way with the open stick, controlling it with the reverse stick and accelerating past the opponent's open-stick side. Again the sudden change of pace and direction should be emphasized.

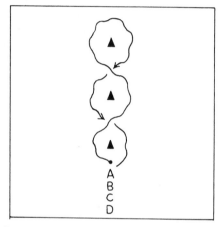

Fig. 25

8. (See fig. 26) Four players and one ball in each grid. Each player dribbles the ball in and out of the obstacles as for 7, but instead of returning back to the start the ball is passed back to the next player. The players continue to practise as long as the teacher/coach requires. A competitive element can be introduced in the form of relays or timed runs.

Beating an opponent

While it is accepted that passing is the most effective way of beating an opponent it is sometimes necessary to use the individual skills of dribbling or dodging to evade an opponent and set up an attack.

3. Beating an opponent through the legs –
'the nutmeg'
The player with the ball should move to
the opponent's open- or reverse-stick side.
As the opponent is committed to either
side the ball should be slipped through
their legs. The attacking player should
then run round the opponent to collect the
ball on the other side. Changes in speed
and direction are once again essential for
this skill to succeed.

4. Using the right boards to beat an opponent
The player with the ball should move in-
field and to the opponent's open-stick side,
drawing the opponent away from the
side-boards.

When sufficient room has been created
the ball should be played against the right
side-boards at a point almost level with the
opponent and on their reverse-stick side.
The attacking player should accelerate
round the opponent's open-stick side and
collect the ball behind the defender.

5. Using the left boards to beat an opponent
The player with the ball should move in-
field and towards the opponent's reverse
stick. When sufficient space has been
created the ball should be played against
the left side boards at a point almost level
with the opponent and on their open-stick
side. The attacking player should accelerate round the reverse-stick side of the
defender to collect the ball.

Practices to develop the skills for beating an opponent

1. Each player with a ball should practise
    moving one way and then change

direction by stepping off the left or
right foot, dragging or pulling the ball
with them as they do so. Emphasize
the need for close control at all times.

2. (See fig. 27) Working in pairs with one
    ball. Each player in turn moves
    towards a static obstacle, such as a
    cone, skittle or block; once they are
    within 2 metres of the obstacle they
    should dodge or dribble round it by
    changing direction and speed. Stress
    the need for good timing and balanced
    footwork.

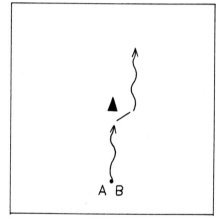

Fig. 27

3. As for 2, but the cone, skittle or block
    is replaced by one of the players who
    provides static/passive opposition
    while their partner dribbles and
    dodges around them.

4. Working in pairs with one ball. Player
    A attempts to beat player **B** who is
    now allowed to tackle but without
    moving his or her feet.

5. (See fig. 28) Player **A** must now at-
    tempt to beat player **B** and get to line

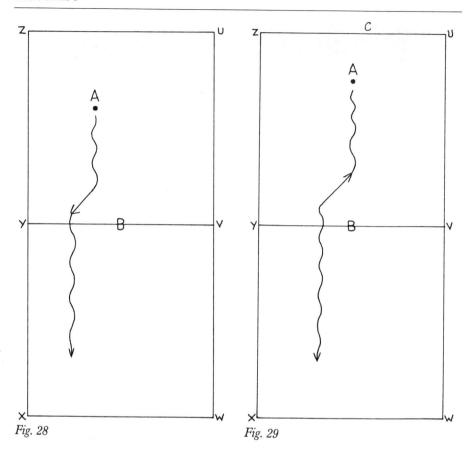

Fig. 28   Fig. 29

WX. Player **B** is allowed to tackle but must remain on line **VY**.

6. (See fig. 29) Working in threes with one ball. Player **A** must try and beat player **B** and reach line **WX** with the ball under control. Player **B** must try and tackle player **A** and if successful must pass the ball to player **C** on line **UZ**.

It is important that the players are asked to practise in spaces which are closely related to the real game of indoor hockey. Too much space is as unsatisfactory as is too little space.

7. All small-sided games with uneven sides, e.g. 2 v 1, 3 v 2, 4 v 3, 5 v 4, 6 v 5, will give players plenty of opportunity to practise these skills.

Running with the ball

There is a significant difference between running with the ball and dribbling. Dribbling, as has been pointed out, requires close control. This in turn means that players should have total concentration on the ball, often to the exclusion of

26

The body and feet: The body is held in a more upright position, making it easier to run at speed and look up while doing so. Good, balanced footwork is once again essential.

The stick and ball: The stick and ball should be kept out in front and slightly to the right of the body. The player should learn to 'carry' the ball like this while running at speed. A pass or shot at goal can be made from this position if necessary.

Running with the ball. Note how the player is using the time and space available to look up and assess the situation before choosing his next move.

everything else that is going on around them. Running with the ball requires players to 'carry' or propel the ball with the stick without any exaggerated or complex movement of the ball. As such this will allow them to look up and assess the situation before choosing their next move.

Running with the ball is most effective when there are no opponents in close proximity to the player in possession and when there is plenty of time and space in which to operate – usually there is no need to dribble past or beat an opponent.

Coaches and teachers should help players recognise when they should dribble and when they should, in fact, run with the ball.

The grip: As for dribbling but with the right hand slightly higher up the shaft of the stick.

Practices to develop running with the ball

1. (See fig. 30) Each player should run around the perimeter of the court, hall or gym with the ball under control on the open-stick side. The players should then sprint down the sides of the court and jog along the ends, and should attempt to look up as often as possible while practising this skill.

2. (See fig. 31) In pairs with a ball each. Player **A** runs with the ball around player **B** and back to the start. Player **B** repeats the exercise. Each player should run round the open- and reverse-stick side of the stationary player.

3. (See fig. 32) In pairs with one ball. Player **A** runs with the ball to the far side, turns and passes to **B**. **A** returns to the starting point while **B** repeats the exercise.

4. (See fig. 33) Four players with one ball. Players **A** and **B** stand on one side of the grid or court and players **C** and **D** on the other. Player **A** runs with the ball to the half-way point and passes to **C**. Player **A** then runs on to

27

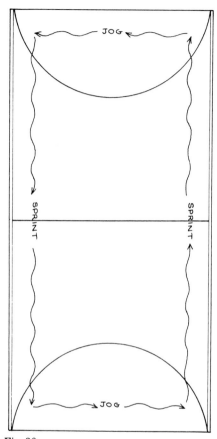

Fig. 30

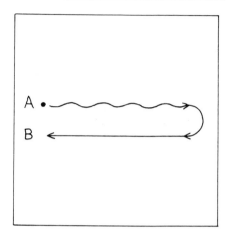

Fig. 32

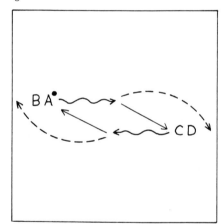

Fig. 33

line up behind **D**. Player **C** runs with the ball to the half-way point and passes to **B**. **C** runs on to join the line behind **B**, and so on for 30 seconds. Add a competitive element by counting how many runs are made in the allotted time.

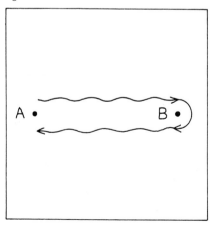

Fig. 31

4

Basic skills – shooting

Shooting at goal is the most important attacking skill and every move in the game is designed to create a shot at goal. It should never be sufficient to be satisfied with the creation of shooting chances; these chances must be converted into shots on target.

All children and older players enjoy the experience of success when shooting. In Chapter 6 games for beginners have been discussed where plenty of opportunities are given to allow players to experience shooting, and achieve high scores. Initially coaches and teachers should allow beginners to experiment with shooting skills to discover which they find most successful and which more difficult to master. As the skill level and experience in indoor hockey develops so it is necessary to help players develop the four main shooting skills, as well as making a decision on:

1. when to take the responsibility to shoot, and
2. when it is better to give a pass to someone who is in a better position to shoot.

There are two situations when a player should refrain from shooting:

1. when the goalkeeper is so close that he/she is certain to block the shot.
2. when the angle is so narrow that the chances of scoring are remote. Shots made from outside the effective shooting area (see fig. 34) are likely to fall into this category.

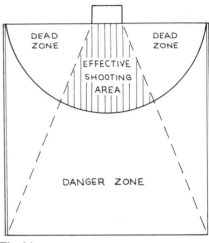

Fig. 34

Every player should:

1. be able to make the decision to pass or shoot;
2. if shooting, be able to choose the correct technique for the circumstances;
3. be able to shoot on target.

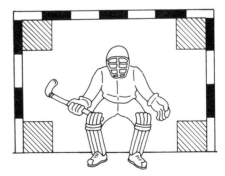

Fig. 35 Target areas.

In indoor hockey players should aim to shoot into one of the four target areas – see fig. 35. Shots along the ground are more difficult for the goalkeeper to save than shots in the air.

As with passing techniques, there are a number of shooting techniques.

A. The slap shot

The 'slap shot' is a development of the 'slap pass' as discussed in Chapter I (see page 8). Beginners may find this the easiest way of shooting as it allows the development of techniques already acquired. It is most effective at all levels of play when there is little time and/or space in the circle, but can result in inaccurate shots, and so it is important that players also learn a more accurate shooting technique as with the flick shot.

The grip: As for the slap pass (see page 8)

Body position: The feet should be ½ to 1 metre apart, the body crouched, and knees bent with body weight slightly over the back (right) foot. The left foot should be pointing roughly in the direction the shot is to be made.

The stick and ball: The stick is held away from the body, with the stick head in contact with the ground. The stick begins a short distance behind the ball, and is brought into contact with it in a sweeping action. The angle at which the stick face makes contact with the ball will determine the height of the resulting shot, i.e. whether the ball will be played along the ground or in the air.

Making the shot: To play the shot along the ground players must place their left foot alongside or just in front of the ball so

that their body weight is directly over the ball at the moment the ball is struck.

The stick is swept along the ground, with the right hand providing the most power and direction.

To play the shot into the air, players must place their left foot 10 cm - 25 cm (approximately 4 inches - 10 inches) behind the ball. The body and stick actions remain the same, while the power of the shot and the angle the stick face makes in contacting the ball will be sufficient to lift the ball into the air.

B. The flick shot

The 'flick' is a skill which allows a player to make a fierce, accurate and lifted shot at goal. It is a technique specifically used for shooting as the indoor hockey rules allow the ball to be lifted only when a shot at goal is being made. With practice, players can learn to place the ball in specific areas of the goal (see target areas page 29), particularly when shooting from penalty corners and penalty strokes.

The grip: As for the push pass, with both hands gripping the stick firmly. In the early stages, players should be encouraged to position the right hand lower down the stick to gain greater control.

Body position: At the beginning of the movement, the body should be crouched with the knees bent and the body weight slightly over the right foot. The feet should be ½ to 1 metre apart, with the left foot pointing in the direction the ball is to travel.

The stick and ball: As with the push pass, the stick is kept in contact with the ball throughout the movement. In order to lift the ball, the stick head is angled away from it so that the edge of the stick can be placed underneath.

Making the shot: In executing the shot the stick should release with the ball in a position alongside or just in front of the left foot. The body weight is transferred from the right to the left foot while straightening the right knee at the same time, so giving added power and lift to the shot.

The follow-through of the stick head will determine the trajection of the ball, i.e. a low follow-through will give a low shot.

The flick shot: *Stage 1.*

Stage 2

Stage 3 Note the angle of the stick head and the position of the ball.

31

Stage 4 Note the follow-through of the stick, and the body weight right over the left foot.

SUGGESTED STAGES IN TEACHING THE FLICK SHOT

In pairs and with one ball and no sticks.

Stage I: Standing 3 - 4 metres apart, each player should in turn step forward, place the left foot by the ball and by bending forward and using the right hand like a scoop, lift the ball into their partner's hands.

Stage II: Using the right hand only to hold the stick in the correct position, players should place the edge of the stick under the ball and gently lift it into their partners' hands. *Stress* the importance of adopting a crouching body position with knees bent to get under the ball and then

Teaching a young player how to flick and lift a ball: *Stage 1*.

Stage 3

straightening the knees when lifting the ball.

Stage III: Repeat Stage II with two hands on the stick.

Stage IV: Dribble the ball forwards and flick it while on the move.

Stage V: Flick a moving ball received from another player.

Stage 5

C. The jab or deflected shot

This shot is peculiar to indoor hockey. Its execution is enhanced by the nature and design of the indoor stick whose sharp, angular edges allow it to be 'jabbed' under the ball with an outstretched arm. It is a more advanced skill relying on the player in possession of the ball making *a hard, accurate pass*. It is particularly effective when made from the right goal post; it is a more difficult skill to perform on the left side.

The grip: The stick is held at the top in one hand only. If the shot is made from the right post then the stick is held in the right hand (left hand for a shot on the other side).

Body position: Players maintain an upright body position allowing them to sprint away from the marker.

The stick and ball: Shooting from the right goal-post – the stick is held in the right hand, with the arm extended, in front and slightly to the right of the player's body. The stick face is angled slightly upwards and forwards (see photograph on page 34) so that it can raise and deflect the ball towards the goal. In other words, the stick is used as a ramp to launch the ball towards goal.

Making the shot: The player making the shot stands 1 - 2 metres outside the right goal-post and near the goal line. They should sprint towards the feeding player with their stick head on the ground to deflect the hard, accurate pass into goal. The player making the pass should aim to pass to the right goal-post.

33

Demonstrating the technique involved in the jab or deflected shot.

D. The scoop or floated shot

The 'scoop' or 'floated shot' is a subtle but advanced skill which, when executed well, results in goals of grace and beauty second to none! It demands high levels of skill and technique together with great concentration and awareness. It is most effective against goalkeepers who come off their lines and spread themselves horizontally to prevent the usual slap or flick shots at goal.

The grip: As for the flick shot.

Body position: As for the flick shot.

Stick and ball: As for the flick shot.

Making the shot: The techniques involved are similar to the flick shot except that the angle of the stick head is more open and more of the stick is under the ball.

The ball is 'scooped' up and over the body of the advancing goalkeeper on a high, curved trajectory towards the goal. Moving from the crouched position by straightening the knees will help to get the necessary lift on the ball.

A further advantage of this type of shot is that it is very difficult to defend by opposing field players, since any player attempting to prevent the ball going into goal will have to make a conscious effort to play it out of goal and will thus concede a penalty stroke.

E. Shooting areas

(See fig. 63, page 53) It is most effective to shoot from the shaded areas within the circles; coaches and teachers should, therefore, try to encourage players to get free to shoot from within this area, preferably with the pass coming from the right making it easier to receive and shoot.

Practices to develop shooting skills

1. Players have one ball each; they slap or flick the ball at a wall in the following ways:
    a By starting with a stationary ball.
    b By dribbling and flicking the ball.
    c By flicking a moving ball received from another player on their right.
2. Players are positioned with one ball each just outside the circle. (See fig. 36)

    A dribbles into the circle and flicks at goal. As soon as the shot is made **B** repeats. This continues until all the players have had a shot; then, balls are collected. 2 shots each are allowed at this station before players change positions:

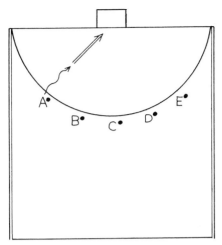

Fig. 36

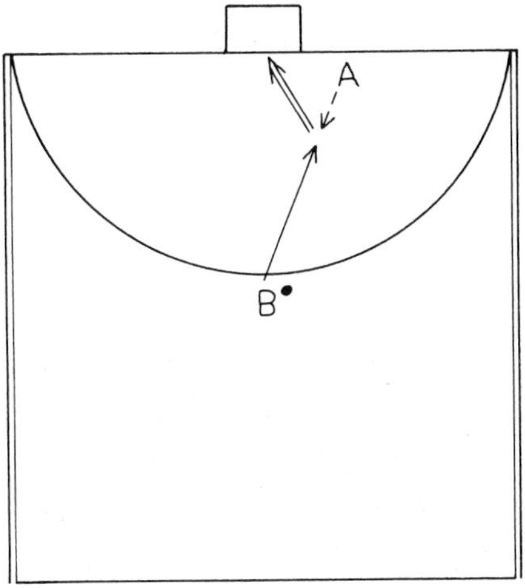

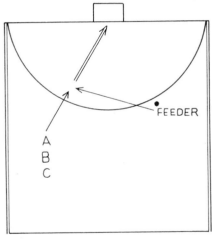

Fig. 37

a Shoot in order **A,B,C,D,E**.
b Shoot in order **A,E,B,D,C**.
3. As for 2, but cones or hoops are put in the four target areas (see fig. 35).

Players are given 10 shots each. 1 point is scored if a shot results in a goal, and 5 points if it hits one of the four targets.

4. Players form pairs and one ball is given to each pair. **A** runs towards **B** who passes, hard and accurately, to inside the right goal-post (from the passer's view point). **A** deflects the ball into the goal with a deflected or jab shot. (See fig. 37)

5. **A**, a player without the ball, accelerates to the circle, a feeder passes the ball and **A** slaps/receives and flicks or scoops at goal. (See fig. 38)

Stress the need for the feeder to pass near the left foot or *slightly in front of* the shooting player.

6. As in **5** with the ball coming from the left and shooting with a controlled flick.

Fig. 38

Emphasize to feeders that they should pass near the right foot, or *slightly in front*, of the shooting player.

7. **A** accelerates with the ball through the cones. As soon as the ball crosses the circle line, **A** should scoop/float the ball into goal. (See fig. 39)

35

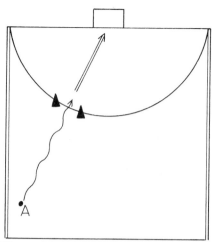

Fig. 39

8.   The goalkeeper shouts 'Go!', sprints to touch the penalty spot, and then crosses to defend the shot from **A**. (See fig. 40)

As the goalkeeper shouts, **A** accelerates through the two cones:

   a if time and space, to make a controlled flick;

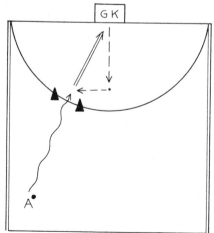

Fig. 40

b if little time and space as goalkeeper slide tackles, to scoop or float the ball into the goal over the goalkeeper.

9.   Vary the angle of shooting; feeders make hard, accurate passes for **A, B,** and **C** to receive and flick/slap into goal. (See fig. 41)

Then they feed to **D, E,** and **F**, collect all balls, and repeat the practice. After this the three groups should change round.

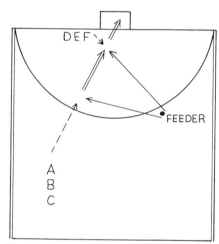

Fig. 41

5

Basic skills – marking

All attacking moves are designed to put the defending team at a disadvantage, thereby creating goal-scoring chances for the attacking team.

The defending side will inevitably be concerned with disrupting these attacking moves by reducing the options available to them. The main aim of the defense is to deny the attacking team a shot at goal, and to regain possession of the ball.

All players must be able to defend well, and a sound understanding of marking is vital to any team. There are two main ways to organise a team's marking:

a man-to-man marking.

b zonal marking.

Although the two marking systems have many different features, it should be noted that there is no such thing as a "straight" man-to-man system or "straight" zonal system. The authors would suggest encouraging beginners to use "tight" man-to-man marking so that players can develop their own individual defensive skills and become aware of their individual responsibilities in a one versus one situation. As skill levels and tactical awareness improve they can be taught to employ "loose" man-to-man marking.

With more advanced players and well organised teams both systems can be utilised according to the particular opposition or phase in a game.

Man-to-man marking

The basic concept of man-to-man marking is that when the opposition have the ball each defender marks an assigned opponent. This can be done by:

1. "Tight" man-to-man marking

This is based upon the close marking of attacking players over the entire court as soon as the opposition are in possession of the ball.

Defending players must:

a stay as close as possible to their opponents;

b make it as difficult as possible for their opponents to receive a pass;

c keep between their opponents and the goal, thus preventing them from passing, dribbling or shooting;

d keep their opponents on their forehand side or open- stick side where they are most vulnerable.

2. "Loose" man-to-man marking

Each defender is still responsible for one opponent but, instead of following them wherever they go, is merely required to stay 2 to 5 metres away *until* the attacker approaches the circle or receives the ball and thus becomes 'dangerous'.

This is a more effective system to operate as defenders do not become so tired and are less likely to be drawn out of position,

37

which in turn means a greater depth and cover in defense.

Defending players must:

a position themselves so that they can see both the opponent they are marking and the ball;

b switch from one attacker to another to avoid being drawn out of position;

c move in tighter to their opponent if they receive a pass, or move near to the defending circle, as in "tight" man-to-man marking;

d not rush in to make a tackle, but must force their opponent into the dead zones (see fig. 34 on page 29).

Switching is a difficult skill and should not be used with beginners or inexperienced players – in general these players should make every effort to stay with their own opponents.

Zonal marking

Zonal marking is based upon the simple idea that goals can only be scored from inside the circle. Therefore, by employing all the defending team to defend the circle (in a similar way to basketball), they aim to prevent the ball entering and thereby reduce and/or eliminate scoring chances by the attacking team.

Defending players must:

a be responsible for defending a particular area (zone) on the court. This is usually in and around their own circle.

b ensure that the opposing player with the ball is 'hustled' so that he/she cannot pass or dribble into the circle but is forced to make a pass or to dribble out and away from the circle.

c position themselves so that all passing channels into the circle are covered and there is depth in defence.

d ensure that opposing players who move into the circle to receive a pass are picked up and marked man-to-man tightly.

e ensure the area around the penalty spot is always covered.

f be capable of adjusting their defensive position (and that of the zone) as swiftly as the attacking side switches the ball from one part of the court to another.

g be capable of switching from zonal marking to man-to-man marking and back again as the situation demands.

h be ready to intercept the ball and counter-attack as soon as possession is gained.

With zonal marking it is helpful if the defender farthest away from the ball (sometimes the goalkeeper) can see all the attacking players and can communicate their movements to the other defenders in the team.

TEACHING ZONAL MARKING

Stage I

One way of introducing players to zonal marking is to teach them to play a half-court man-to-man system.

a When possession is lost, all defending players retreat to the half-way line.

b Defending players then man-to-man mark the opponents when they cross the half-way line.

When the players have mastered this half-court semi-zonal man-to-man system they may progress to a full zonal system.

Stage II

a Mark chalk circles, 6 metres in diameter (see fig. 42) on the court to show the areas to be defended by each player. The centres of the circles should be the defenders' starting positions.

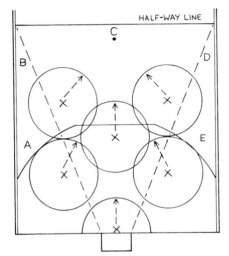

Fig. 42

b Attacking players **A**, **B**, **C**, **D**, and **E** position themselves in a semi-circle outside the defensive zone.

c The central attacker, **C**, has the ball on the half-way line.

d The defenders move to the edge of their respective circles in the direction of the ball.

e The ball is moved to another attacker so that the defenders have to adjust their positions to cover the ball by moving to the edge of the circle nearest it.

f Attackers continue to move the ball between them while the defenders swiftly adjust to cover all possible channels for passes into the circle.

g Defenders must also be aware of the positions of players off the ball and be ready to man-to-man mark any players entering the shooting circle.

Stage III

a Develop Stage II so that the attackers attempt to score and move into the circle.

b Defenders adjust the Stage II positioning to a more realistic situation and mark attacking players moving into the shooting circle.

Successful zonal marking depends on team understanding and talking to cover all possibilities of passes into the shooting circle, and on man-to-man marking of attacking players entering the shooting circle.

Attacking players should find they have two defenders to beat before they can make a shot at goal and must, therefore, endeavour to get as many players as possible forward to overcome the zonal marking. This in turn leaves the team open and vulnerable to swift counter attacks by the defending team as soon as the latter gain possession.

Getting free from a marker – creating space to receive a pass

The aim of the attacking team is to create space and time in which they can pass and receive a ball, and so build up an attack.

Since the defending team aim to put pressure on the attacking side by trying to restrict the amount of space and time available to them, all players must learn to get free to receive a pass, especially where they will be a threat to the defending team, in other words, *near or in the attacking circle.*

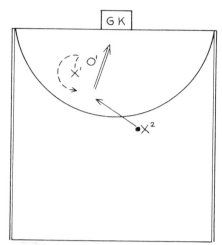

Fig. 44

USING CHANGES OF DIRECTION AND SPEED

a X^1 is tightly marked by O^1; X^1 walks towards the goal and his marker O^1, then *suddenly* turns and sprints in the opposite direction to receive a pass from X^2. On receiving, X^1 can:

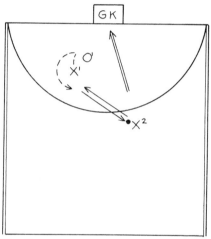

Fig. 43

(i) give the ball straight back to the free player X^2 to shoot (see fig. 43)
(ii) cut in on the reverse-stick side of O^1 to shoot (see fig. 44)

b X^1 is tightly marked by O^1. X^1 walks towards the circle edge; O^1 will follow. X^1 *suddenly* turns in towards O^1 while X^2 passes into the space for X^1 to receive and shoot. (See fig. 45)

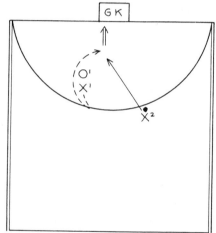

Fig. 45

c Similar to a basketball or lacrosse roll – X^1 stands close to the marker with his/her back to it. X^1 suddenly rolls around to the right, staying close to O^1 to receive a pass from X^2 in the space. X^1 receives and shoots. (See fig. 46)

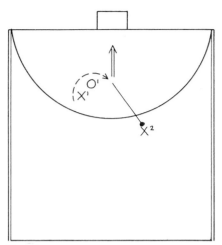

Fig. 46

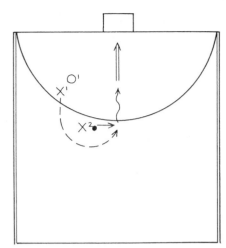

Fig. 47

d Looping or overlapping – clear communication between the player making the overlap and the player in possession is essential. **X**^{1} accelerates away from the tight marker, **O**^{1}, and loops behind **X**^{2} who passes the ball to **X**^{1} to receive and shoot. This is difficult for **O**^{1} as this player has to follow behind or lose **X**^{1} in the loop. (See fig. 47)

Additional teaching points

1. Encourage players in possession to pass to marked players who are accelerating to lose their markers.
2. Passes should be made at the *correct pace*, i.e. fast enough so that the advantage gained by the player getting free is not lost, but still affording the receiver ease of control.
3. Passes should be made at the *correct angle*, either onto the moving player's stick, or into the space so that the receiver has as wide a vision as possible of the situation.

4. Passes should be made at the *correct time*, giving the receiver sufficient time to control the pass and make the next move, but not enough for the defender to recover.

Practices to develop all aspects of marking

Good footwork, with the ability to make sudden changes of direction and speed, is an essential skill for achieving success in marking and losing an opponent. All practices therefore, with or without a ball, are most valuable.

1. Cones or bibs placed at varying distances down the court. Players practise without a ball but carry their stick; they should alternate walking/jogging with sprinting.
2. As in example 1, but as a shuttle (see fig. 48), i.e.
   Jog to station 1 → 2, sprint back to 1.
   Jog to station 1 → 3, sprint back to 2.

Jog to station 2 → 4, sprint back to 3.
Jog to station 3 → 5, spring back to 4.
Jog to station 4 → 6, sprint back to 5.
Jog to station 5 → 6, sprint back to 1.

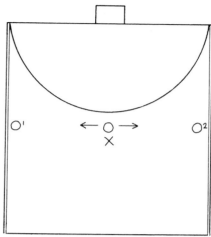

Fig. 49

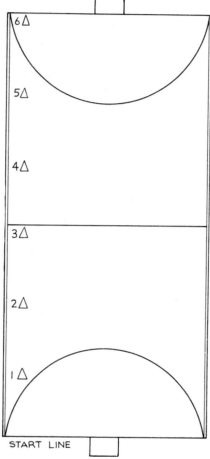

Fig. 48

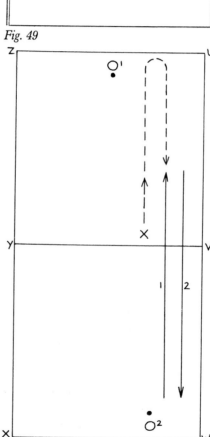

3. Players practise in twos without a ball, but they should hold their sticks. They stand in the centre of the court, facing each other. **O** suddenly accelerates to **O**¹ and **X** tries to keep

Fig. 50

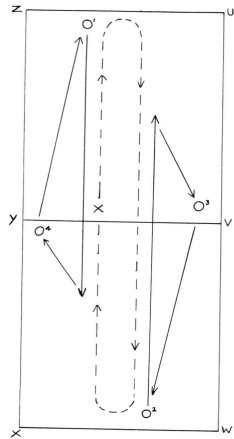

Fig. 51

with **O**; or, **O** turns quickly to accelerate to O^2 and **X** again tries to keep with **O**. **O** can introduce a feint and sprint or walk a few paces to wrong-foot the marker. (See fig. 49)

4. Threes and two balls. O^1 and O^2 have a ball each. **X** sprints towards O^1, turns quickly on the line **UZ** to accelerate and immediately receives a pass from O^2; **X** then passes the ball back to O^2 straight away, continues running and turns quickly by O^2 to receive a pass from O^1. This practice

may continue for 10 to 20 turns after which players change roles. (See fig. 50)

5. Fives and two balls. As in **4** except that on receiving the pass from O^2, **X** passes to O^3, and on receiving from O^1, **X** passes to O^4, i.e. **X** passes to the *left* – the easier side. O^3/O^4 return the ball to O^2/O^1 respectively.

6. Repeat **5**, with **X** passing to a player on the right. (See fig. 51)

7. Threes and one ball to a grid; two cones/another player/mark on the wall. O^2 has the ball. O^1 aims to lose marker **X** in any way possible, O^2 must pass with the correct angle and pace and at the correct time for O^1 to receive. O^1 and O^2 then work together to pass the ball through the cones. (See fig. 52)

8. As in **7**, with the player **O** to the right of the grid.

Small sided games of 2v1, 3v2, 4v3, 4v4, 5v5 (Roller Ball, Consecutive Hockey) as discussed in Chapter 6 (see pages 51 and 52) will give plenty of opportunities for players to develop their marking skills.

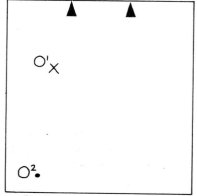

Fig. 52

6

Introducing the game to beginners

As soon as players acquire the basic skills of passing, receiving, dribbling and shooting at goal, they become keen to try these skills out in the game situation. While it is important for this development to take place, many teachers and coaches make the mistake of allowing beginners to play a full game too soon. As a result, the players find themselves in a game which, although full of action, is full of mistakes and frustration – a game in which everyone chases the ball and one or two players, because of their natural ability, monopolise play to the exclusion of the other less able players, the very ones who need the practice.

Nothing is guaranteed to discourage, dishearten and disappoint a young player more than the isolation and frustration that this sort of game can create. Furthermore, this situation makes it extremely difficult for the teacher/coach to analyse what is going on. It is usually impossible to isolate aspects of play and correct appropriate skills, or to maintain the interest and enjoyment of the players.

Where then does the teacher/coach start when introducing the game to beginners?

Small-sided games and *conditioned games* form a very useful link between pure basic skill practices and the full game. Small-sided games offer players of *all* abilities the opportunity to be more involved in the game, so giving them more opportunity to improve their skills and techniques. Condi-tioned games will concentrate play on a particular skill or technique that the teacher or coach wishes to develop. Together they offer the teacher/coach the opportunity to develop individual skills and tactical awareness in every player. This, through purposeful and concen-trated practice, makes for an efficient team unit.

Small-sided games and conditioned games, like basic skill practices, should always be realistic and related to the full game. If well designed they can be *purposeful, enjoyable* and *successful* for the players. In fact, if the 'conditions' are created correctly, then learning should take place, even without direct formal teaching or coaching.

These games should have:

1. *Few rules* – allowing players to get on with the game without the frequent interruptions that would normally occur.

2. *High scoring potential* – so offering the players the opportunity to achieve high scores which emphasise and rein-force the positive aspects of the practice.

3. *Plenty of action, excitement and fun*

The questions that now face the teacher and coach are:

1. What to practise and coach?
2. How to practise and coach it?

In general these small-sided and condi-tioned games can be grouped into:

1. Games that emphasise attacking play, and
2. Games that emphasise defensive play.

It is important for the teacher/coach to structure the sessions so that the players are offered the opportunity to practise those aspects of the game which are essential to success in the full game.

Success at Indoor Hockey is based on scoring more goals than the opposing team or, alternatively, conceding fewer goals. Practices that encourage attacking moves and the scoring of goals will do as much to enhance the confidence and development of players as will the coaching of sound defensive skills and tactics.

Inevitably the length of the sessions and the aspects that have to be developed will depend upon the age and the ability of the players involved. The following practices are intended to give teachers and coaches an idea of how a series of small-sided games and conditioned practices can be put together to help in the development of any aspect of attacking and defensive play. All the practices can and have been used with players of all abilities, from beginners to international players.

As a rough guideline, an indoor hockey lesson or coaching session can be structured on the following lines:

1. Age – 8-11 years
Time – 45 minutes, broken down into:
Warm-up – 5 minutes
Basic skill practices – 15 minutes
Small-sided and conditioned games and practices – 15 minutes
Period of small-sided free play (allied to full game) –10 minutes

2. Age – 11+ years
Time – 60 minutes, broken down into:

Warm-up – 5 minutes
Basic skill practices – 15 minutes
Set piece practices – 10 minutes
Small-sided and conditioned games and practices – 15 minutes
Period of small-sided free play (allied to full game) – 10 minutes.

3. Club players
Time – 60 to 90 minutes, broken down into:
Warm-up – *10 minutes*
Basic skill practices – 20 minutes
Set piece practices – 20 minutes
(More time, say 30 minutes, can be devoted to either basic skills or set pieces depending on the amount of concentrated practice the teacher or coach wishes to spend on these areas.)
Period of small-sided/uneven-sided or full-sided free play – 20 minutes.

Small-sided and conditioned game practices

I. Two versus one

Attacking play

X^1 stands with the ball on line **WX**. X^1 and X^2 must try and score a point by stopping/trapping the ball on the line **YZ**. Defender O^1 has to try to prevent them from doing so. (See fig. 53)

The options open to X^1 at the start are:

a To take on and beat O^1 and to score.

b To run at O^1, commit the defender and pass to X^2 to score.

c To exchange passes with X^2 until O^1 is drawn out of position and a gap appears which allows either X^1 or X^2 to score.

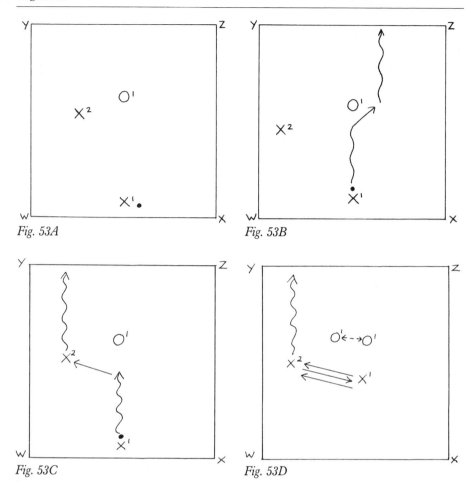

Fig. 53A Fig. 53B

Fig. 53C Fig. 53D

Defensive play

O^1 must try to prevent X^1 and X^2 from scoring. He or she must also attempt to gain possession by tackling or intercepting the ball.

The first objective will be to take up defensive positions which reduce the attacking options available to X^1 and X^2 to a minimum. For example, when X^1 has the ball on the left hand side of the pitch (as the defender sees it), O^1 should close X^1 down in a way that allows X^1 only two attacking options:

  a to dribble or dodge past O^1 on the reverse-stick side, or

  b to pass to X^2 on O^1's open-stick side.

By overplaying *one* of these options O^1 can tempt X^1 into taking the other and, with good anticipation, can bring off a tackle or interception to gain possession of the ball (see fig. 54). Similarly if X^2 has the ball on the right hand side of the pitch (as the defender sees it), O^1 can move across to cover any run by X^2 down that side and so tempt X^2 into making a pass to X^1. Again, with good timing and anticipation, O^1 can gain possession of the ball (see fig. 55).

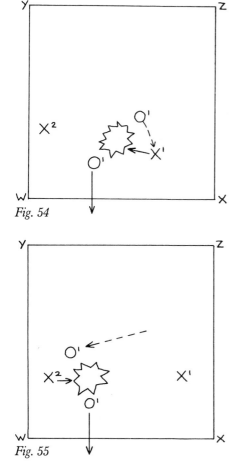

Fig. 54

Fig. 55

Conditions

As the players improve, various conditions can be imposed on the attackers and the defenders, e.g.

1. X^1 and X^2 must make three passes before being allowed to score.
2. O^1 must not only gain possession but must also pass the ball over line **WX** to score a point.
3. O^1 must now pass the ball to a team-mate, O^2, who is confined to line **WX**. (See fig. 56.)

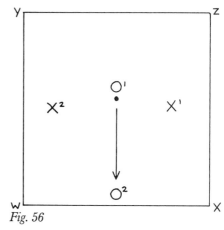

Fig. 56

2. THREE VERSUS ONE
Attacking play
X^1 starts on the line **WX**. X^1, X^2 and X^3 must attempt to score a point by stopping/trapping the ball on line **YZ**. Defender O^1 must try to prevent them from doing so (see fig. 57).

The introduction of the extra attacking player will offer the player on the ball more options with which to beat O^1. It does, however, also present the problem of deciding which option to choose. Quite often the safest pass will not be the most effective one. The most effective one, on the other hand, might involve more risk. For example (see fig. 58) if X^1, passes to X^2, O^1 will have time to recover. A pass to X^3

47

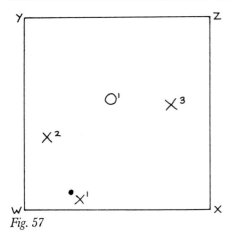

Fig. 57

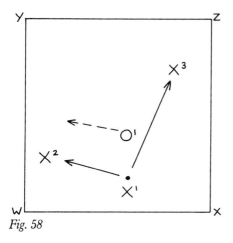

Fig. 58

will lead to a scoring chance but there is a risk of the pass being intercepted if it is not a good one.

Practices such as this, together with good teaching and coaching, will help players improve their tactical awareness and basic skills.

Defensive play

O^1 now has more options to cover; nevertheless, O^1 must attempt to take up defen-

sive positions that delay the attack (this will help the defending team in the full game). He or she must also try to force the attacking team to move the ball into areas where they will have fewer options open to them. (See figs. 54 and 55)

Conditions

1. X^1, X^2 and X^3 must all touch the ball before they can score.
2. The attackers are only allowed to play 'two-touch' hockey.
3. The attackers must score in 10, 20 or 30 seconds otherwise they lose a point.
4. If the ball touches O^1's feet the attackers get a point.
5. O^1 gets 5 points if he/she gains possession and passes the ball over line **WX**.

3. THREE VERSUS TWO
Attacking play

The practice is similar to Practices 1 and 2. The introduction of a second defender, O^2, will force the attackers to work together more effectively to create scoring opportunities.

1. If X^2 and X^3 are closely marked they will have to move to draw their markers, O^1 and O^2, out of position and so create space for X^1 to move in to score (see fig. 59).
2. X^1 can also try to commit one of the defenders to the tackle and pass the ball to the free attacker to score (see fig. 60).

Lateral, diagonal and overlapping runs can all be used to tempt defenders out of position and create scoring opportunities for the attacking team.

Note must be made of the need for cover

to be provided while attacking just in case possession is lost and a quick counter attack is set up.

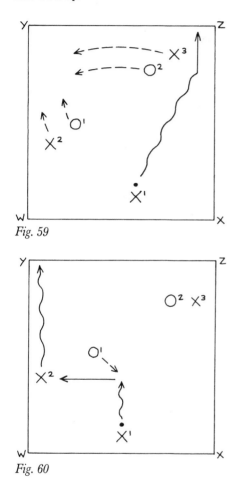

Fig. 59

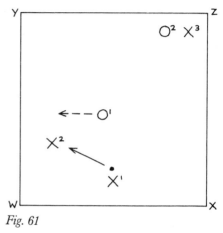

Fig. 60

Defensive play

This is an excellent opportunity to introduce players to the skills of man-to-man and zonal marking.

If O^1 and O^2 choose to man-to-man mark the players off the ball, they may be drawn out of position by the players they

are marking, so allowing the third attacker space in which to attack the line **YZ** and score. They must try to adopt a system, therefore, which slows down the attack and forces the play away from line **YZ**. To do this they will need to mark tightly any attacker who threatens the line. Attackers further away from the line will be marked loosely or zonally.

Fig. 61

For example (see fig. 61), if X^1 has the ball, O^1 will find a position that prevents X^1 from attacking **YZ**. X^3, who is nearest to the line, is marked tightly by O^2 while X^2, who poses no real threat or danger, is left relatively free. If the ball is passed to X^2 then O^1 will move to cover any attempt by X^2 to attack **YZ**, leaving X^1 comparatively free. As long as O^2 can prevent X^3 from getting the ball, O^1 can attempt to force X^1 and X^2 into areas where the available attacking options become less effective.

In this practice the three attackers should always succeed in beating the two defenders. It is surprising how often this does not prove to be the case.

49

Conditions
As in practice 1 and 2. The practices can be developed further by:
Stage 1: Introducing specific targets or goals in which to score.
Stage 2: Increasing the number of players involved to 4 v 2, 5 v 2, 5 v 3, thereby increasing their attacking and defensive options.

4. CONTINUOUS THREE VERSUS TWO INDOOR HOCKEY

This is a small-sided, conditioned game which can be used to involve all the players in the group and still provide the teacher or coach with an opportunity to isolate various aspects of play, correct skills, and develop tactical awareness.

Each team (up to 15-a-side can be used) lines up on the goal line to the left of their own goal, with the exception of the goalkeepers who stay on the pitch throughout the game. X^1, X^2 and X^3 start by attacking the goal defended by O^1 and goalkeeper O (see fig. 62). The normal rules of indoor hockey apply for the attacking team, unless the teacher or coach wishes otherwise. The defender involved (in this case O^1) may use any part of his or her body or stick to tackle, intercept and gain possession of the ball. This condition is imposed at the outset to encourage the attacking players to play *round* and *not through* defenders. It can be changed at the teacher's or coach's discretion so that eventually the normal rules of indoor hockey apply to the defenders as well.

The moment a goal is scored, or the attackers make a mistake or lose possession, they must clear the pitch and retreat to their own goal line as quickly as possible.

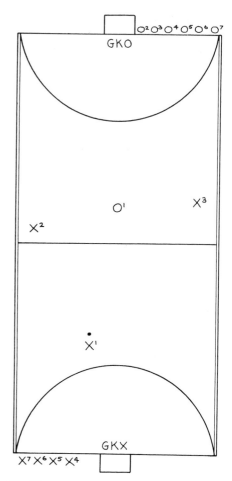

Fig. 62

Defender O^1 is immediately joined by O^2 and O^3 and sets out to attack the opposition goal which will now be defended by X^4 and goalkeeper X. If the O team score a goal, make a mistake or lose possession they must immediately leave the pitch and retreat to their own goal line while X^4 attacks the opposition goal joined by X^5 and X^6; defender O^4 and goalkeeper O must prevent them from scoring, and so on.

This is an excellent exercise for:

1. *Developing attacking play*
   a Finding the unmarked player
   b Playing round defenders
   c Building quick counter attacks
   d Shooting at goal
2. *Developing defensive play*
   a Tackling and intercepting
   b Covering and marking
   c Closing down
   d Reducing options
   e Providing goalkeeping practice
3. *Developing fitness*
   The players work continuously.
4. *Maintaining concentration*
   The players on the line must be prepared to come into the attack the moment possession is gained or to defend the moment possession is lost.
5. *Involvement*
   Every player is involved all the time during the exercise, both physically and mentally.
6. *Teaching and coaching*
   Because it allows the teacher/coach to observe all the players in both attacking and defensive roles it presents an ideal opportunity to analyse and assess the all-round ability of each individual more effectively.

It also allows coaches to impose appropriate conditions on the players at any time to make them learn and develop those skills and techniques which are essential to success in the full game − ultimately, the aim of all teachers and coaches is to transfer what one has coached in small-sided, conditioned games to the full game. By progressing steadily from 2 v 1 to the 6-a-side game with realistic and relevant practices the probablity of achieving this will be maximised.

Quite often the final step can present the greatest obstacle and games such as Roller Ball, Consecutive and Non-stop Hockey can form an important link at this stage.

ROLLER BALL

3 v 3, 4 v 4, or 5 v 5 in half a court. Utilise extra players as umpires/scorers. One tennis ball or slightly larger rubber ball is required, and no sticks. Put upturned forms across the middle and ends of the half gym, giving two areas bounded by four walls. If this is not possible use the side walls/sideboards to pass off, and lines at the ends as boundaries.

Objectives

1. To keep possession.
2. To create passing (scoring) chances.
3. To introduce marking/losing a marker.
4. To make positive use of available space.
5. To introduce passing off walls/sideboards.

Rules of roller ball

1. The ball can only be passed by rolling it along the floor.
2. If there are only two walls/side-boards, when the ball goes over the side lines a free roll-in should be awarded to the opposition.
3. The side walls/side-boards may be used to pass off.
4. Score by counting consecutive passes before the opposition touch the ball.
5. The player with the ball may travel in any direction, but the main objective is for the other players in the team to move into space and lose their markers to receive a pass, or to create space for other team members to receive a pass.
6. Begin the game with one player in

possession of the ball, who rolls it to another team member.

7. There should be no contact. The opposition gain possession either by intercepting or when the opposition lose the ball over the side lines.

Teaching points to develop during the game of Roller Ball

1. Encourage good use of space and the avoidance of crowding near the player with the ball.
2. Encourage each player to take responsibility for marking one of the opposition.
3. Help players to lose their markers – initially, by drawing away from the player with the ball, then suddenly accelerating into a space to lose the marker and to receive a pass.
4. Encourage the players to keep moving to give the player with the ball a choice of passes.

Consecutive Hockey

In this game the players use their sticks. The rules are similar to those of Roller Ball. Scores are achieved by making consecutive passes before the opposition gain a touch of the ball.

Initially, condition the game to no tackling to give the player with the ball time to make accurate passes, and time to the supporting players to move to receive passes. As the players become more skilful, lift the condition of no tackling so that the supporting players and the player with the ball have less time and space in which to react.

Objectives

1. To develop scoring ability.
2. To develop a game more closely related to the full game.

Non-stop Hockey

3 v 3, 4 v 4 or 5 v 5, 6 v 6.

Initially only a minimum of rules – mainly ones regarding safety – including no barging and no dangerous tackling. Goals can be adapted by using benches, cones, skittles or marks on the walls.

At this stage players will understand the basic skills of passing and receiving, and although other aspects of the game, both skills and tactics, may be introduced, it is best at first to allow the players to shoot from anywhere, to turn on the ball, and to kick it accidentally, etc. This encourages continuous play; the ball never goes 'out' and it is played off all four re-bound walls/side-boards.

At the outset the main aim is to reduce the number of stoppages. It is up to the teacher/coach to step into the game and isolate those aspects of play to be improved. Where necessary appropriate skills should be corrected and developed, but the enjoyment of and continuity in the game must be maintained.

Teaching points to develop in Non-stop Hockey.

1. Sensible spacing using all the area. Encourage players to move away from the player with the ball. This will create space for them to accelerate into to receive a pass or for another team member to receive a pass.
2. Encourage all players to work hard to support any team-mate who has the ball, i.e. to move to create a choice of pass.
3. When attacking one player should always be left in defence – the anchor man who positions to cover any counter attack.

4. When the opposition are in possession of the ball, all the defending team should assume a defensive role.
5. Use of the walls/side-boards to pass should be encouraged.
6. Accurate passing gives more time and space for the player receiving the pass to dribble, pass or shoot.
7. When defending encourage players to close opponents down effectively, to time their tackles rather than rushing in, and to intercept passes.

As the players' skills, techniques and tactical appreciation improve, more rules can be introduced until a *full game* or *near full game situation* is reached. However, even at this stage it should not be assumed that the need for small-sided, conditioned games no longer exists.

Learning and developing indoor hockey skills is a continuous process which needs regular coaching and rehearsal in order to reinforce and perfect them. It is important that all lessons and coaching sessions include frequent, if only short, periods of small-sided and conditioned play interspersed with basic skill practices and periods of full free play.

The full game

Possible points to consider when developing the full game:
1. Continue to develop points 1 - 7 of *Continuous Hockey*.
2. Introduce a correctly attired goalkeeper (see Chapter 9) as soon as possible and stress their complete involvement in the game.
3. Develop individual roles.

4. When a team is in possession get four players in attack, with preferably three in or very near the attacking circle, leaving the GK and one defender guarding the central area of the court, ready for a counter-attack.
5. Try to get the ball into the middle of the court where more options are available.
6. Develop looping behind the player with the ball, again to open up more options.
7. Stand still with the ball if no good passes are available and wait for team members to create opportunities. Pass the ball back or square, keeping possession while waiting for chances to open up.
8. Develop some ideas as set pieces (see Chapter 8) but always allow an individual to assess a situation and use flair to create scoring chances.
9. See fig. 63. Try and get the free player and the ball into the shaded area for

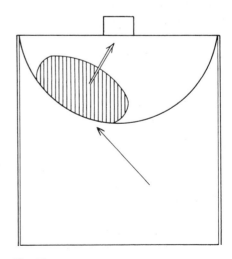

Fig. 63

the shot, as it is far easier to make a good shot from this position.

10. Practise defending/attacking corners (see Chapter 8) so that individual strengths are exploited and players are very clear as to their individual roles.

11. Everyone should practise penalty strokes.

Supplementary small-sided games and conditioned games

These are useful to develop certain skills and tactics:

1. Hockey/Cricket (see fig. 64)

Two teams of 4, 5 or 6, using four grids, a badminton court or half a hall area according to available space.

Batsmen **A, B, C, D** and **E** in turn dribble the ball round cones 1 and 2. Every time a player and ball get to cone 1 one run is scored. Fielder, **F**, begins with the ball, which is passed around the team. When the ball returns to **F** 'Change!' is shouted

and the next batsman from **A, B, C, D** and **E** comes in. The exercise is repeated until every batsman has had a turn. The teams change over – the winning team is the one scoring the most runs.

Skills practised:

a dribbling, keeping close control

b accurate, quick passing

c passing the ball clockwise and anti-clockwise

2. Hockey/Rounders (see fig. 65)

4 v 4, 5 v 5, 6 v 6; half a hall is used.

A, B, C, D and **E** are batsmen and **F, G, H, I** and **J** are fielders.

F gently passes the ball to **A** who can stop and clear it, or clear it first time. **A** then immediately sprints to the spare ball at cone 1 and dribbles/runs with the ball at speed round the cones until cone 6 is reached. The fielders aim to collect the cleared ball and get **A** out by scoring a goal before **A** passes the last cone. If **A** does pass the last cone before a goal is scored **A** scores a rounder.

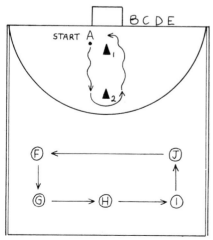

Fig. 64

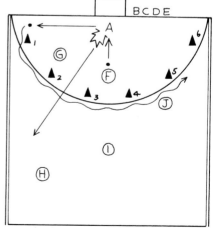

Fig. 65

According to time available, allow 5 minutes batting time for each team, or three goes for each batsman.

When goalkeeping skills have been introduced, a GK can defend the goal, making it even more difficult for the fielding team to score.

Skills practised:

   a batsmen placing their clearance

   b dribbling at speed

   c fielders creating scoring chances quickly

3. 3 v 2 + Umpire

Using half or the whole hall, depending on space available to develop disciplined defence.

4. 4 v 4 + Umpire

For this game 9 players and one ball to four grids (a third of a netball court, half a full indoor court) are required (see fig. 66).

Players can use the side-boards to pass (use upturned forms to create more side-boards). Teams score 2 points if they score through their opponents' goal, or 1 point if they make three consecutive passes before an opposing player touches the ball.

Develop:

   a positive spacing

   b support for the player with the ball

   c tight marking

   d losing marker

   e accurate passing

   f receiving under pressure

As players become more skilful introduce a GK to each team.

5. 3 v 2

Use half an indoor court/hall/gym. X^1, X^2 and X^3 begin with the ball on the half-way line and attack the goal defended by O^1 and **GK O**. O^1 and **GK O** must prevent them from scoring. They must also try to:

   a gain possession by tackling or intercepting

   b pass the ball over the half-way line.

X^1, X^2 and X^3 should be encouraged to:

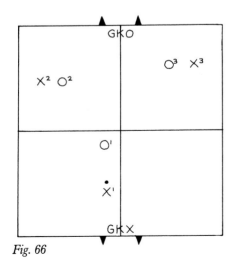

Fig. 66

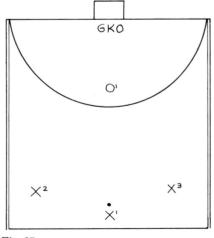

Fig. 67

55

a move to create space

b give choice of pass to the player in possession

c loop behind the player in possession

d bring the ball into the middle of the court

e develop quick passing

f get a free player into the shaded area to shoot (see fig. 67).

6. 3 v 2

Use the whole court (see fig. 68). Objectives to develop are:

a a quick counter-attack, particularly from a zone defence

b a quick recovery from attack to defence

X¹, **X**² and **X**³ start at the top of their own circle. **O**¹ faces the opponents' goal line and shouts 'Go!'; the three attackers **X**¹, **X**² and **X**³ aim to score a goal. Defence **O**¹ must recover quickly to help **GKO** to prevent them from doing so. If **GKO** or **O**¹ gain possession they must attempt to get the ball over the half-way line. Initially, have few rules so that play is continuous, but pay attention to safety at all times. The game continues until **X**¹, **X**² and **X**³ score a goal, or **GKO** and **O** succeed in passing the ball over the half-way line.

7. 3 v 1 and 3 v 2

Use the whole court as above.

This is an exercise which can be used to involve more players and to practise more skills than in any game previously mentioned. Player **X**¹ stands at the top of the near circle with the ball. **X**² and **X**³ stand on the half-way line near the top of the far

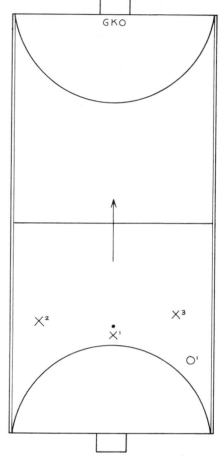

Fig. 68

circle (see fig. 69). **O**¹ stands on the penalty spot behind **X**¹. On the command 'Go!', **X**¹ passes to **X**² and sprints to the far circle. **X**² passes to **X**³ who passes to **X**¹; the latter should be in or arriving in the far circle from where he or she will shoot at goal.

O¹ will also start on 'Go!', sprint to the far circle after **X**¹ and try to prevent **X**¹ from shooting at goal by tackling **X**¹ or intercepting the pass from **X**³ to **X**¹. The moment a goal is scored by **X**¹, or a tackle or interception is made by **O**^{1}, **X**^{1} must clear the pitch and return to the start. Meanwhile **O**^{1} sprints back to the penalty spot from which he or she started to prepare for another defensive run with **X**^{4}

Conditions

1. Introduce a goalkeeper to defend the far goal.
2. **O**^{1} is permitted to tackle and intercept any of the passes between **X**^{1}, **X**^{2} and **X**^{3}.
3. Two-touch hockey.
4. **O**^{1} must gain possession of the ball and clear it over the half-way line.
5. **O**^{1} takes **X**^{3}'s place after 4, 6 or 8 runs and so must perform basic stopping and passing skills in a state of tiredness.

The teacher/coach can create a number of situations in which the skills and techniques of the players can be tested to the full. To underestimate the capabilities of the players is to miss the whole point of coaching which is to improve the ability of the players in as many aspects of the game as possible at any one time.

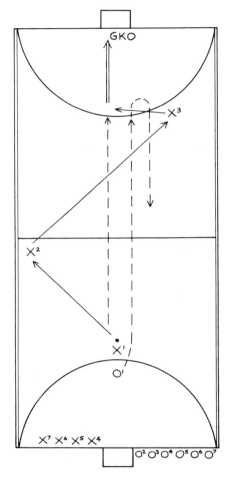

Fig. 69

who is ready to repeat the exercise carried out by **X**^{1}.

The defender **O**^{1} and feeders **X**^{2} and **X**^{3} are replaced after 4, 6 or 8 runs.

7

Elementary tactics and the development of the game

Creating space

Players in possession of the ball need space in which to operate. Without it they can be closed down, hurried into their next move or forced into making errors and consequently losing possession. Players with good basic skills need less space in which to operate than players with poor skills.

Space is created by co-ordinated team play and is exploited by individual players. It is possible for individual players to create and exploit space for themselves, but unless their skills are used in harmony with the rest of the team they will find themselves isolated and will be a handicap to both themselves and their team.

Space can be created in two main areas of the pitch:

  a in the middle, and
  b on the flanks.

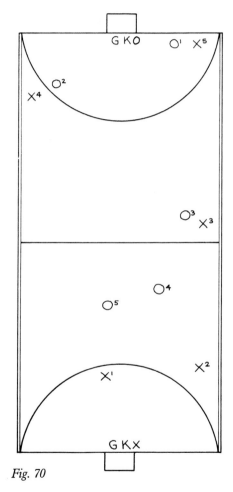

Fig. 70

CREATING SPACE IN THE MIDDLE OF THE PITCH

Attacking players can create space in the middle of the pitch, especially near the opposition's circle, by spreading out and moving towards the side-boards and corners (see fig. 70). This will draw defenders apart and create space between them which can then be attacked and exploited.

CREATING SPACE ON THE FLANKS

Attackers can do this by moving towards the middle of the pitch in or near to the op-

position's circle. This will draw the defenders together, thereby creating space on either side of them which can be attacked and exploited (see fig. 71).

58

Space can also be created on either flank, depending on which side of the pitch the team in possession wants to build its attack. This can be done by getting the attacking players to move to one side of the pitch, so drawing their defenders with them. This will create space on the opposite side in which to build an attack (see fig. 72).

When used with quick changes of pace and direction, attacking moves like this present defenders with enormous problems.

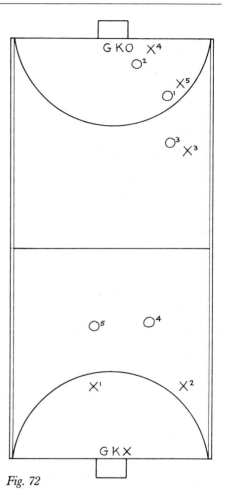

Fig. 72

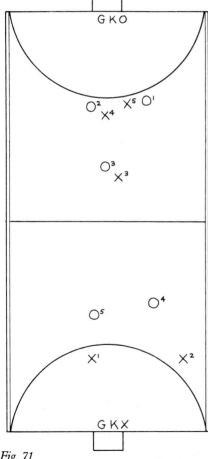

Fig. 71

Firstly, they are drawn out of their normal lines of defence, and secondly it creates uncertainty in the minds of the defenders. They have to decide:

1. how close they should stay to the attacker they are marking;
2. whether they should mark the player or the space; or
3. whether they should provide cover for the defender marking the player with the ball.

USING 'BLIND-SIDE' RUNS TO CREATE SPACE

Runs behind defenders, or 'blind-side' runs as they are sometimes called, are particularly unsettling for defenders.

1. They force defenders to turn and watch the attackers they are marking to the exclusion of the ball and the build-up of play. As such they are unable to anticipate the attacking moves of the opposition or to provide cover for beaten defenders in their own team.

2. If the defenders choose to watch the ball to the exclusion of their opponents they will be unaware of the movements or the position of the attackers on the pitch, so making it easier for the attackers to find, create and exploit the space available. Attackers who play up and down the pitch in straight lines assist defenders in their marking and covering.

Sadly, space created by the quick thinking and movement of players off the ball is often lost by the poor skills of the player on the ball. Teachers and coaches must be aware of this and make players realise that for the maximum advantage to be gained from the possession of the ball and the creation of space certain points must be observed.

1. *The quality and timing of the passes must be good.* They must be given fast enough to take advantage of the space created and allow the receiver to control the ball easily yet prevent the defender from recovering.

2. *Selecting the right pass is also important.* The player on the ball must be able to decide on the line of best advantage, i.e. whether the ball should be played into the space or to the receiver's stick.

3. *Passes should be made in a way which allows the receiver as wide a field of vision as possible at the moment of control.* The receiver must continue to be aware of the build-up of play and be able to decide on the next move early and without excessive pressure from the opposition.

Players not directly involved in the build-up of play should work to keep their markers busy so that it is impossible for them to give depth or cover to the defence.

Support play

Once the defending team discover the direction in which the attack is being built up they will attempt to stop play developing in that direction: to continue to attack in that direction, especially against good defenders, is both risky and foolish. They will do this by closing down the player with the ball, so reducing the space and options available. In this situation the players off the ball should be alert to what is happening and should move to support the person with the ball so that they can pass the ball sideways or backwards. Players cannot be considered to be in supporting positions if they are not in a position to receive a pass (see fig. 73). Players must realise that it is sometimes necessary to move the ball sideways, or even backwards, before progress forwards can be made, even when play is near the opponents' circle (see fig. 74).

Supporting distances can and do vary according to which part of the pitch play is taking place. The nearer the one is to the

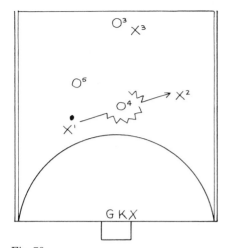

Fig. 73

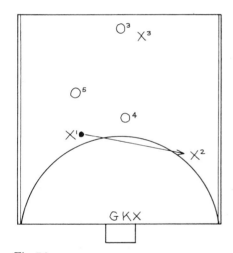

Fig. 74

attacking half to 5-10 metres in the defending half.

Support for the player with the ball can be provided by players in forward positions moving back towards their own half, or by players in defensive positions staying where they are or moving forwards at the right time (see figs. 75 and 76).

Unfortunately players who receive passes in good supporting positions are often tempted to use the time and space created to dribble or run with the ball instead of us-

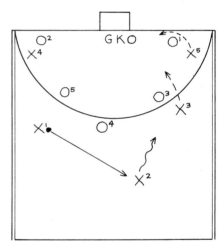

Fig. 75

ing it to make an effective pass. Teachers/coaches should help players to realise the disadvantages of dribbling or running with the ball:

1. It takes longer to run with the ball from point **A** to point **B** than to pass it.
2. Defenders have more time to recover.
3. There is the inevitable loss of vision because of the concentration required for keeping the ball under control.

opponents' circle the less space there is, the more defenders there are and the more tightly attackers are marked. There is usually more space, fewer defenders and looser marking away from the opponents' circle. The distance of support required will therefore vary from 2-5 metres in the

61

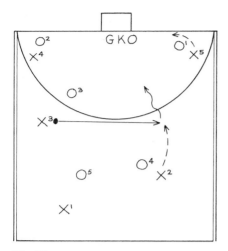

Fig. 76

4. Options are reduced as the player is forced to run into the dead zones on the pitch.

Practices which help players to develop an awareness of the state of play are essential when coaching team tactics. From this basic awareness players will begin to synchronise their movements and skills to help each other as a team unit.

Practices

Two-touch hockey

This practice is designed to encourage players off the ball to give the player on the ball the correct type of support when necessary to beat the defending players.

1. Five **X** players (the attackers) play against two **O** players (the defenders).
2. In each circle and confined to the circle there is a target man, G^1 and G^2 – this can be the goalkeeper.
3. No outfield player is allowed into the circles at any time.

4. At the start of the game the **X** players have possession and must combine to score a point by passing to G^1.
5. After a point has been scored G^1 must immediately pass the ball back to an **X** player, and play continues with the **X** team again combining to score a point by passing to G^2 at the other end. The ball cannot be played back to G^1 when the **X** team are attacking the target man G^2, and the same rule must apply to G^2 when they are attacking G^1. This ensures that the **X** players move all around the pitch to support each other. (See fig. 77)
6. The **O** players must try to prevent the **X** team from scoring points and should attempt to score points for themselves by making tackles and intercepting passes.

The purpose and development of this game
There are four phases to this game.
1. In phase one players are allowed only two touches of the ball each time they get possession – the first time to control the ball and the second time to pass it or score.

This condition places great emphasis on basic skills and highlights the passing and receiving techniques of individual players. Footwork and vision are also highlighted and improved.

Players off the ball soon learn to 'read' the game and appreciate the options open to the player on the ball immediately it is received. They should, as a result, learn to support quickly and effectively. The player on the ball also learns to choose the correct option and the line of best advantage when passing.

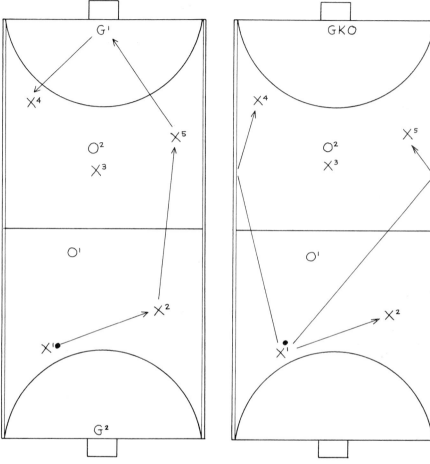

Fig. 77   Fig. 78

Because the attackers outnumber the defenders there are always one or more attacking options available to the player on the ball. The players will soon learn to choose the correct option and the line of best advantage when passing (see fig. 78).

As the players' skills and tactical awareness improve the second and third phases can be introduced.

2. The attacking players are now allowed just one touch of the ball. This forces players to find much more space in which to operate; this, in turn, makes them 'read' in advance what options are open so that they can exploit them with their first touch.

3. The number of defenders (**O** players) is slowly increased so that greater

63

pressure can be put on the attackers, thereby reducing the space and options available to them. The attackers should be allowed to return to two-touch hockey during this phase.

4. Both sides have an equal number of players. The two-touch and scoring conditions are lifted and full indoor hockey is played, with normal rules applying.

The teacher/coach can, if necessary, re-introduce the two-touch condition for one or other of the sides to develop a particular aspect of the game. If this is done it is usually a good idea to reduce the number of players on the opposing side so that the game is allowed to flow and is not beset by errors.

Building an attack down the right

All attacking play is designed to create shooting opportunities in the opposition circle. Because hockey is predominantly a right-sided game most tactical play has concentrated on building attacks down the right-hand side of the pitch.

There are a number of reasons for this.

1. It is usually easier to beat an opponent on the reverse-stick side.
2. It is easier to pass from right to left.
3. It is easier to shoot quickly when passes are received from the right.

Attacks can be built down the right in three main ways.

1. By passing directly to attacking players in forward positions.
2. By overlapping and making runs from deep positions.
3. By using the side-boards to create the extra player.

PASSING DIRECTLY TO ATTACKING PLAYERS IN FORWARD POSITIONS

1. Player X^1 passes to X^4 who takes on and beats the opposite number on either the open- or reverse-stick side, and shoots (see fig. 79).

2. Player X^1 passes the ball into the space on the right-hand side of the pitch for X^4 to pick up on the reverse-stick side, beat the opponent and shoot (see fig. 80).

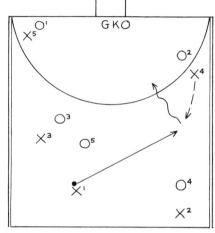

Fig. 79

These attacking moves are most effective when there is space for the players receiving the ball to dribble or pass into. It should be understood that players who can turn quickly in a confined space are most effective in these situations. They can force defenders into making mistakes when play is in these areas.

3. Player X^4 receives a pass from X^3 who makes a supporting run on the blind side of O^3, receives a return pass from X^4, proceeds into the circle and shoots (see fig. 81).

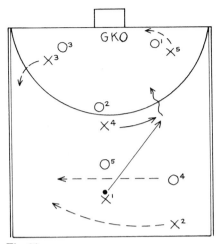

Fig. 80

The position in which **X**⁴ receives the ball is very important. This player should receive the ball in a position that allows him/her to see the supporting run of **X**³. If **X**⁴ is closed down so that there is no space to dribble or pass into then he/she should

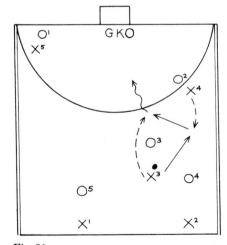

Fig. 81

not attempt to get the ball to **X**³ but should aim to pass the ball back to **X**¹ or **X**² who should be providing the deep support essential in all attacking play (see fig. 82).

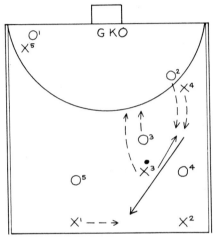

Fig. 82

OVERLAPPING AND MAKING RUNS FROM DEEP POSITIONS

Overlap runs should always be made behind the player with the ball so that support is provided on the outside and square, or slightly forward, of the player with the ball. Overlapping runs are most effective when there is space for the supporting player to move into. When there is no space in which to operate then the supporting player should stay behind to offer the player with the ball the option of a pass back or square.

Clear communication between the player in possession and the overlapping

65

player is essential. Quite often a call like 'Hold it!' is enough to make the player in possession realise what is happening and wait for the run by the supporting player.

1. Player X^1 passes to X^2 who moves inside with the ball. X^1 'loops' round behind X^2, receives a pass from X^2 and builds an attack down the right-hand side of the pitch (see fig. 83).

2. X^2 passes the ball to X^1 and makes a diagonal run towards the opposition circle. X^3 times the run to coincide with this move, looping round X^1 to receive a pass in the space created by X^2's run (see fig. 84).

3. X^2 passes to X^3 who plays the ball into the space between O^3 and O^4 for X^2 to run onto and build an attack (see fig. 85).

There is always some risk involved in overlapping and making runs from deep positions, and care should be taken that the

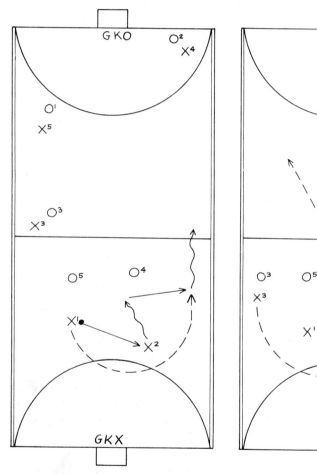

Fig. 83

Fig. 84

66

team is not left outnumbered and without cover at the back if possession is lost. At the same time there is no point in continuing to provide cover for the player with the ball if there is a good opportunity for the supporting player to move forward and build an attack. Other players should move to provide cover.

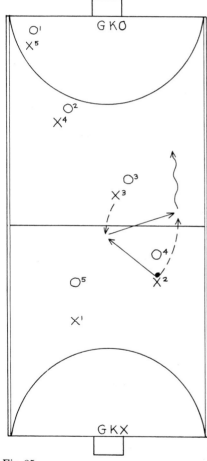

Fig. 85

USING THE SIDE-BOARDS TO CREATE THE OVERLAP

In indoor hockey it is possible to use the side-boards to build an attack.

There are three main ways in which this can be done:

1. By playing a long pass into the opposition half or circle for players in a forward position to receive and use.

    X^2 uses the side-boards to pass the ball into the space created on the right-hand side of the pitch for X^4 to run onto and receive (see fig. 86).

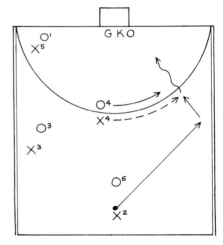

Fig. 86

2. By playing a short pass to another player and making a supporting run to receive a return pass.

    X^3 uses the side-boards to pass to X^4, makes a supporting run on the blind side of O^3 and receives a return pass from X^4 (see fig. 87).

3. By using the side-boards to make a pass to oneself – the 'Ego' pass.

    X^2 moves inside, drawing O^4 away from

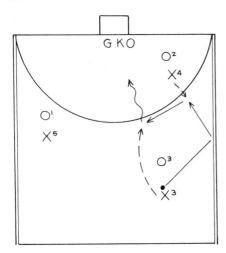

Fig. 87

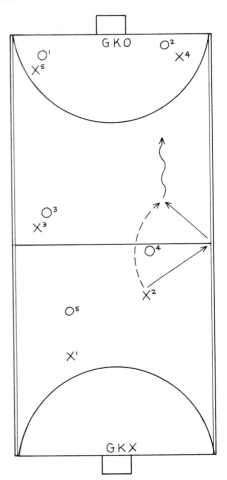

Fig. 88

the side-boards and committing O^4 to tackle on the open-stick side. The ball is then played onto the boards past O^4's reverse-stick side with sufficient pace and angle to allow X^2 to run round and pick up the ball behind O^4. It is important that the ball is played off the boards at a point level with the opposing player to create the correct angle of rebound (see fig. 88).

In every instance it is important for the player making the pass to create enough room between the opponent and the side-boards to get the ball through. If there is insufficient room, the pass will almost certainly be intercepted.

Players should never attempt to beat two opponents down the boards with a single pass. Players in forward positions can help by positioning themselves so that they are in front of the second line of opponents if a pass down the boards is anticipated (see figs. 87 and 88).

Defending against attacks down the right

When a team is defending, the object is to put pressure on the attacking team by restricting the amount of time and space available to them. If it is more effective for teams to build attacks down the right-hand side of the pitch, it falls upon the defending team to endeavour to prevent this from happening.

The first step towards achieving this aim is to ensure the correct positioning of the player marking the ball. A defender who stands square on to the attacker with the ball leaves himself/herself open to attacks down his/her left, the attacking team's right. The defender marking the person with the ball should overplay the cover to the left (reverse-stick side) by positioning himself/herself so that his/her right foot is lined up with the right foot of the attacker. This will make it more difficult for the attacker to beat the defender on the reverse-stick side and will force the attacker to try to dribble or pass down the defender's open-stick side where tackling and intercepting is easier.

Clear communiction between the covering defenders and the player marking the person with the ball is essential. Directions to 'move left' or 'move right' will help the player to find a position that helps the covering players and at the same time puts pressure on the player on the ball.

Should the defender marking the ball be beaten on the reverse-stick side, they should initially force the attacker to stay close to the side-boards so that the player is forced into the corners or 'dead zones' where there is less space and fewer options available. If the beaten defender attempts to tackle back, it should be carefully executed with no risk of committing an offence. It is often best for the beaten defenders to retreat to the penalty spot immediately and leave the covering defenders to confront the attacker with the ball. As defending players retreat towards their own penalty spot they automatically reduce the time and space available to the attacking team.

Building an attack down the left

If the attacking team's efforts to attack down the right are impeded, then they must have the ability to change the direction of play and build an attack down the lef-hand side of the pitch.

Once again the attacking options are:

1. *To pass directly to players in forward positions* (see fig. 89). X^1 passes directly to X^5 who takes the ball on the open-stick side and runs round the reverse-stick side of O^1 before shooting.

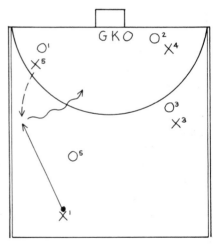

Fig. 89

2. *To overlap and make runs from deep positions* (see fig. 90). X^2 passes to X^3 and 'loops' behind to receive a return pass in the space on the left.

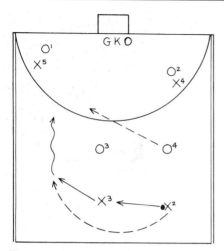

Fig. 90

Defending against attacks down the left

The defending team can prevent most attacks down the left being effective by:

1.   Making sure that there is adequate cover for the defender marking the player with the ball.

     If **X³** beats **O³** then **O²** should be correctly positioned and prepared to move across to cover the break and challenge **X³**. **O³** should retreat to the penalty spot and look to pick up **X⁴** as soon as possible. The **GK** can also help by moving to mark **X⁴** if necessary (see fig. 92).

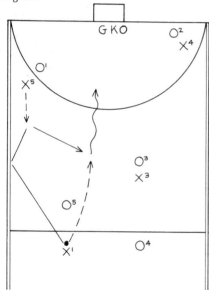

Fig. 91

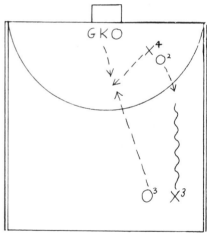

Fig. 92

2.   Forcing attacking players who break away with the ball to make their runs down the side-boards into the 'dead zones'. Tackling back is easier and safer on this side (the open-stick side), but care must be taken not to over-run the attacker who may be looking to try

3.   *To use the side-boards to create the overlap* (see fig. 91). **X¹** uses the boards to pass to **X⁵**. **X¹** makes a supporting run and receives the ball from **X⁵** before going on to shoot.

Defending against attacks down the left. Note how the defending player (in the dark skirt) is standing in a position from where she can see both the player she is marking and the ball.

to cut back inside on the defender's reverse-stick side.

3. Marking all attackers in or near the circle very tightly. Defenders should mark the attackers in a way that they will allow them to move forward to make tackles and interceptions on their open-stick side. They must avoid having the ball played behind them off the boards.

8

Set pieces

The attacking team should have a series of set-piece variations to employ according to the situation – these should be simple and direct and therefore more likely to succeed.

The defending team can only try to anticipate what is going to happen, making it difficult to defend set pieces. Each player must be alert, disciplined and committed to their task to put pressure on the attacking team and in so doing force them to make a mistake.

Push-back from the centre spot

The push-back:
– is used to start a game and to restart after half-time.
– is also used to restart after a goal has been scored.
– can offer the team pushing back immediate possession of the ball.

Example A
In this example X^1 pushes back to X^5 and runs round the 'blind side' of O^1 forcing him to turn and so lose sight of the ball. X^2 and X^3 start their runs on the far side of the pitch, thereby drawing defenders O^2 and O^3 away from the ball. O^4 will move to cover X^4. X^5 will draw O^5 towards him/her and then play the ball off the boards into the space behind O^5 and O^1 for X^1 to run onto and collect. The attacking team will now gain possession in a

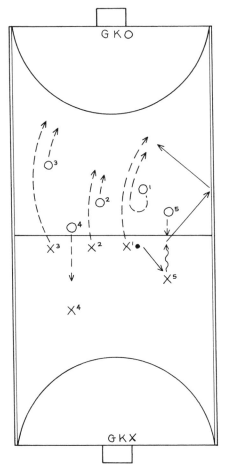

Fig. 93

potentially dangerous area for the defending team. (See fig. 93)

72

Example B

In this example **X**[1] again passes the ball to **X**[5] who this time is standing much closer to the half-way line. Immediately he gets the ball, **X**[5] sprints towards **O**[5] and dribbles round him into the space behind **O**[5] which will have been created by other players in **X**[5]'s team running off the ball. It is the element of speed, surprise and good team work that will create the advantage for the attacking team here. (See fig. 94)

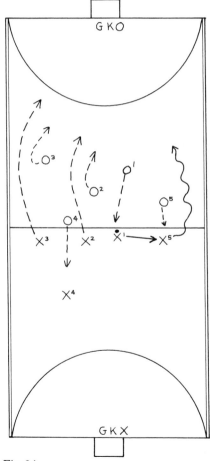

Fig. 94

Penalty corners

Many games of indoor hockey, especially those where the two teams are evenly matched, are decided on the effective execution and defence of penalty corners. Most teams today practise and have at their disposal a variety of drills, both in attack and defence, which they can call upon and apply according to the game's needs.

IN ATTACK

A. Standard penalty corner (from the left with hand-stop)

The most commonly used technique is this one, where the ball is pushed out by **X**[1] from the left side of the goal (as the attacking team see it), and is hand-stopped by **X**[2] at the top of the circle for **X**[3] to shoot. This technique relies heavily on the ability of **X**[1] to push the ball out accurately and fast. The hand-stopper must not only be capable of dealing with fast, accurate push-outs but also with inaccurate ones as well. The hand-stop can be performed with the left or right hand. (See fig. 95)

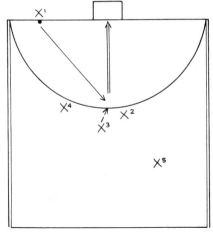

Fig. 95

Penalty corner from the left with hand-stop.

Variation 1A

X^1 pushes out, X^2 hand-stops, X^3 slips the ball to X^4 who shoots. X^1 should move in towards the near post to put the defence under pressure. (See fig. 96)

Variation 2A

X^1 pushes out, X^2 hand-stops and X^3 pushes the ball back to X^1 who shoots. X^1 should move into a better shooting position after pushing the ball out. (See fig. 97)

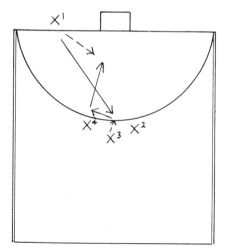

Fig. 96

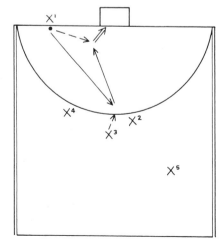

Fig. 97

B. Standard penalty corner from the left (with stick-stop)

If a team does not have a player who is capable of pushing out accurately, or a good hand-stopper, then a stick-stop may be used. This allows for a greater margin of error on the push-out but it does demand excellent basic skills on the part of the stick-stopper.

The procedure is the same as with the hand-stop with X^1 pushing out, X^2 stick-stopping and X^3 shooting. (See fig. 95)

Variation 1B

The ball is slipped by X^3 to X^4 who shoots. X^1 should once again move towards the near post. (See fig. 96)

Variation 2B

The ball is passed by X^3 to X^1 who shoots. (See fig. 97)

Variation 3B

X^1 pushes out, X^2 stick-stops, X^3 feints to shoot but the ball is slipped by X^2, the stick-stopper, to X^4 who shoots. This variation is best used by more experienced players.

C. Stick-stop with three at the top

Once again, if a team lacks a player who can push out fast and accurately or a good hand-stopper then this drill can be used. It allows for a greater margin of error at the push-out and offers the attacking team more options when making a shot at goal. When using this variation the hand-stopping position is dispensed with and X^2 takes up a position further over to the right of X^3. X^1 now has the option of passing directly to X^2, X^3, or X^4, all of whom can shoot directly at goal or slip the ball to any one of the other players around the circle to shoot. (See fig. 98)

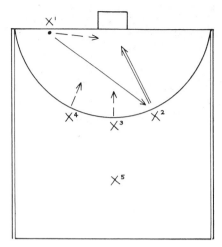

Fig. 98

In every case, player X^5 positions himself to cover any mistakes by his team-mates or any swift counter attack by the opposition if no goal is scored and they get possession.

D. Penalty corner from the right

More and more teams now use the penalty corner taken from the right of the goal (as the attacking team see it) to very good effect. The advantage of taking the corner from this side is that after receiving the ball the shooter does not need to make too many adjustments to feet and body positions before shooting. Corners taken from this side are also difficult to defend as the defending team must attempt to challenge for the ball on their reverse-stick side.

It is difficult to use a hand-stop when the corner is taken from this side, therefore a stick-stop is used. (See fig. 99)

Variation 1

X^1 pushes out to X^2 who shoots.

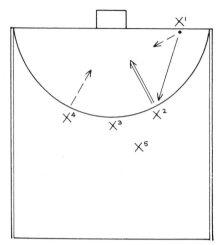

Fig. 99

Variation 2
X¹ pushes out to **X**² who slips the ball to **X**³ who shoots.
Variation 3
X¹ pushes out to **X**³ who shoots.
Variation 4
X¹ pushes out to **X**⁴ who shoots.
Variation 5
X¹ pushes out to **X**², who passes back to **X**¹; **X**¹ then returns the ball to **X**² after moving towards the goal to shoot.

DEFENDING PENALTY CORNERS

The over-riding principle in defending penalty corners is to allow the goalkeeper a clear view of what is going on. Whenever possible no one should run across the goalkeeper's line of vision. In general, most teams line up in the following fashion when defending a standard penalty corner taken from the right of the goal (as the defending team see it) (see fig. 100). The way in which the defending team run out to defend the corner will depend primarily on whether the goalkeeper decides to stay in the goal or run out to confront the shooter. In each case the goalkeeper must make his/her intentions known to his/her team so that they have time to organise themselves accordingly. The goalkeeper is responsible for making saves, while the primary object of the players running out is to force the attacking players to hurry shots and passes.

If the goalkeeper decides to stay, he/she should move off the goal line 1 or 2 metres to narrow the angle for the shooter. **O**¹ should run out to cover any pass to, or shot from, **X**⁴. **O**² should run out to rush or block the shot from **X**³. **O**³ should run out to cover any attempt by **X**² or **X**³ to move into the space on the left of the circle. **O**³ should also be prepared to support any fast breaks and counter attacks by his/her own team if they get possession. **O**⁴ should move into goal to cover the area by the near (left-hand) post. **O**⁵ should move to cover any saves by the goalkeeper or **O**⁴ and clear the ball out and away from the danger area (see fig. 101)

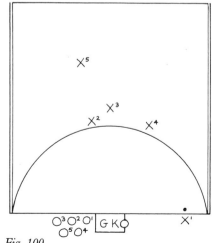

Fig. 100

Variation 6

If the goalkeeper decides to run out to block the shot at a standard penalty corner taken from the right, then this is what the defending team should do. The goalkeeper should run out to block the direct shot at goal by X^3. O^1 runs out behind the goalkeeper to prevent passes to and shots by X^4. O^2 follows the goalkeeper and covers the area to his/her left, so preventing X^2 and X^3 moving into it. O^3 moves out to cover the area behind the goalkeeper and O^2. O^3 should be prepared to clear any saves made by O^4 and O^5 and also be prepared to support any fast breaks and counter-attacks by his/her own team when they get possession.

O^4 must attempt to get across to the far (right-hand) post to cover any shots at goal and prevent X^1 from receiving the ball. O^5 must attempt to get into the goal to cover the area by the near post. (See fig. 102)

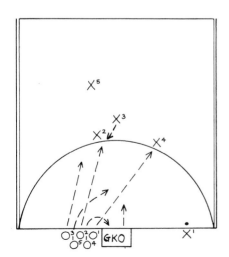

Fig. 101

STICK-STOP, THE GOALKEEPER STAYING

When defending a penalty corner taken from the right to one of three attacking players at the top of the circle who intend to use a stick-stop, then this is what should happen.

The goalkeeper should stay in the goal. O^1 must run out to X^4. O^2 must run out to X^3. O^3 must run out to X^2. O^4 must move to cover the area by the near post. O^5 should cover the area in front of the goal. (See fig. 103)

PENALTY CORNERS FROM THE LEFT

Penalty corners taken from the left of the goal (as the defending team see it) present defenders with the added difficulty of having to challenge and defend with the reverse stick. This can be both difficult and dangerous. Because of this many coaches believe it is best if the goalkeeper runs out to challenge the first receiver and shooter. The goalkeeper's main aim is to prevent **X** from dragging the ball in towards the goal to shoot. **GK** must try to force the first receiver to hurry the shot or pass the ball. If the ball is passed **GK** should try to get across to block the shot from the next attacker. It is important, therefore, that the goalkeeper stays upright while making the challenge.

Assuming then that the ball is pushed to X^2 then O^1 must run out to prevent X^1 from receiving a return pass. O^2 must run out to prevent X^3 from receiving a pass or making a shot. O^3 must run out to prevent X^4 from receiving a pass or making a shot. O^4 must attempt to get across to the far post to cover that side of the goal while O^5 must move into the goal at the near post. (See fig. 104)

Should the goalkeeper decide to stay in the goal then the following moves should be made to defend the corner.

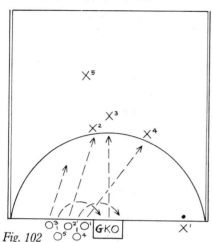

Fig. 102

O¹ must attempt to get across to challenge **X²**. **O²** must challenge **X³**. **O³** challenges **X⁴**. **O⁴** must run out to cover passes to and shots by **X**. **O⁵** moves into the goal to cover the near post. (See fig. 105)

In every instance the goalkeeper must attempt to cover the area of the goal furthest away from where his team-mates start their defending runs.

Free passes

ATTACKING – NEAR THE OPPONENTS' CIRCLE

1. Whenever possible the free pass should be taken quickly. This will deny the defending team time to regroup and organise their defence. It will also take advantage of any lapse in concentration by the defending players after the whistle is blown.

2. If it is not possible to take the free hit quickly the attacking team should then prepare to set up a more controlled and well-rehearsed set piece aimed

Fig. 103

at producing the maximum advantage for themselves.

3. The aim of any free hit taken near the opponents' circle should be to create an opportunity for a direct pass into the circle followed by a shot at goal.

78

4. Each player in the attacking team should be aware of this and should work to create this situation for the player on the ball. The player on the

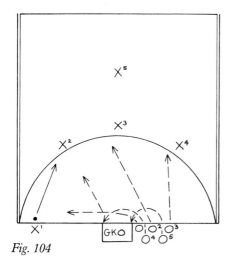

Fig. 104

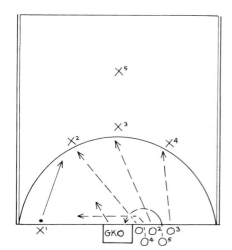

Fig. 105

ball has the responsibility of deciding what type of pass needs to be made

and to whom. To do this he must be aware of team-mates' movements as well as the positioning of the opponents marking them.

5. Inexperienced players often get confused when faced with the option of having more than one team-mate moving free at the same time.

6. Most players can only cope with the decision to pass to one team-mate at any one moment.

7. The coach, through constructive practices, can help develop an understanding between his players so that in the final instance the correct move will be executed.

8. The weighting of the pass is vital. If the ball is passed too quickly there is a risk that the receiver will not be able to control it. On the other hand, if it is passed too slowly the defenders will have time to move in and intercept.

9. The accuracy of the pass is crucial so that the player can start the next move, be it an immediate shot, dribble or pass to another team-mate. Any delay because he/she has to reposition himself/herself or the ball due to a poor pass will give the defenders time to recover.

10. The receiver needs to make sure that the player on the ball is in position and ready to pass before moving in to receive it.

11. It is often possible for the potential receiver to assist the player on the ball by signalling or by calling out when and where the ball is wanted.

12. For free hits to be successful the whole team has to work, with quick thinking and movement, to create space in the

area where the receiver wants the ball.

13. Changes of direction and 'blind side' runs are particularly unsettling for defenders. These force the defending players to turn and watch the attackers they are marking to the exclusion of the ball, or if they choose to watch the ball, they must do so to the exclusion of the attacking players and will as a result allow them to get free to receive the ball.

Three examples of how a free hit situation can be exploited to create space in the opposing circle for a shot at goal are given – see figs. 106, 107 and 108. Coaches will no doubt be able to create a number of additional moves for themselves and their teams.

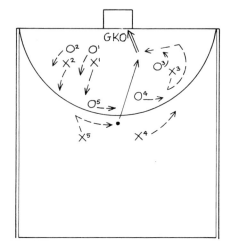

Fig. 106

Push-out from inside one's own circle

These are usually awarded when the ball has gone out of play over the goal line or, occasionally, for offences by players from the opposing team in the circle. If possible this free pass should also be taken quickly, but every care should be taken that possession is not lost. If there is any risk of possession of the ball being lost, then a more controlled free hit situation should be set up.

The main aims at this set piece should be:

1. To retain possession of the ball.
2. To get the ball away from the immediate danger area of one's own circle.
3. To get the ball into the opponents' half at the earliest opportunity.
4. To get the ball into the opponents' circle at the earliest opportunity.

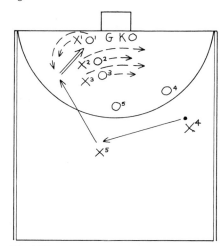

Fig. 107

The points which apply to passing and receiving the ball in all free hit situations should be observed.

1. Passes should be made at the correct time and pace to achieve the best results, i.e. so that the receiver has time and space in which to control the pass and make the next move before the defender can recover.

80

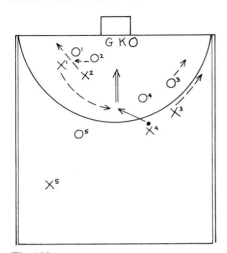

Fig. 108

2. The receiver should adopt a good position to observe the state of play and should be able to move at the correct time and into the correct space to receive the pass.

3. Movement off and without the ball is essential to the success of a team's set plays. In most cases the player on the ball will be faced by an opponent whose main aim will be to prevent the ball from being played forward. The ball must therefore be passed across the circle to someone in a better position to make a forward pass. The opposing players will, of course, move to cover the position of the ball – if the ball is moved quickly back and forth the opposing players will also have to alter their positions to cover the point of attack. Since the ball travels more quickly than the players a space will eventually be created through which a pass forward can be made. (See fig. 109)

The players in forward positions on the

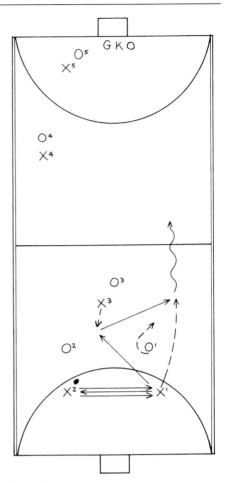

Fig. 109

pitch can help the player on the ball by creating space into which the ball can be played.

They can do this by:

1. Starting their runs from one side, deep in the opposing circle. This has the advantage of:

   a Drawing defenders out of their normal positions and into unfamiliar territory.

b Making it difficult for defenders to watch both the ball and the player at the same time (defenders will have to watch one to the exclusion of the other). (See fig. 110)

c Creating large areas of space into which the ball can be played. The strikers can move back towards their own goal to receive the ball or they can move across the pitch to do so.

2. Starting their runs from the top of the opposing circle. This has the advantage of:

a Crowding out this area, so obscuring the goalkeeper's view of the ball and the build-up of play.

b Allowing strikers more options, i.e. they can move to either side to receive the ball; they can move towards their own goal to receive the ball; they can turn to receive the ball behind the defenders on the opposing goal line.

c Creating more problems for defenders who are forced to cover more options and therefore find it difficult to anticipate the strikers' movements. (See fig. 111 and 112)

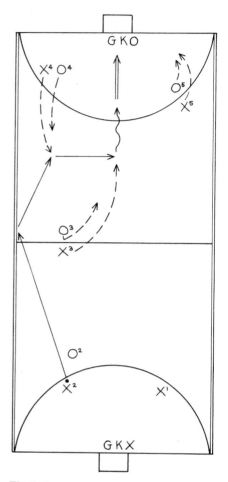

Fig. 110

DEFENDING A PUSH-OUT FROM THE OPPOSING TEAM'S CIRCLE

This will depend to a large extent on the type of marking system being employed by the defending team. If a tight man-to-man marking system is being used, then each defending player will (a) stay as close as possible to their opposite number, and (b) shadow every move and deny them space and time in an effort to prevent them from receiving a pass from the player on the ball.

The person marking the player on the ball has the responsibility of making sure that he/she is not beaten by a pass or a dribble. He/she should also try to force a mistake from the player on the ball by closing down and thereby forcing the attacker to protect the ball. In so doing, the player on the ball will have to concentrate hard on the ball and may find it difficult to assess what is going on around. When a player is

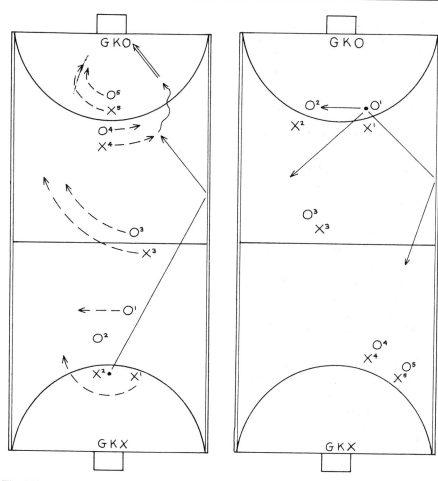

Fig. 111

Fig. 112

isolated in this fashion, they can usually be forced into making a mistake. (See fig. 112)

If a half-court zonal system of marking is used, then the attacking team will be allowed possession of the ball in their own half. The defending team will attempt to position players on the half-way line in such a way that prevents the ball from being played into their own half and circle. The forward defenders should endeavour to win

possession by intercepting passes and setting up quick counter-attacks. Opposing players who move into the defending half and circle should be tightly marked, so making it difficult for the player on the ball to pass to them safely. (See fig. 113)

This system allows the attacking players time and space in which to play their passes, and relies heavily on excellent basic skills, outstanding team work and

83

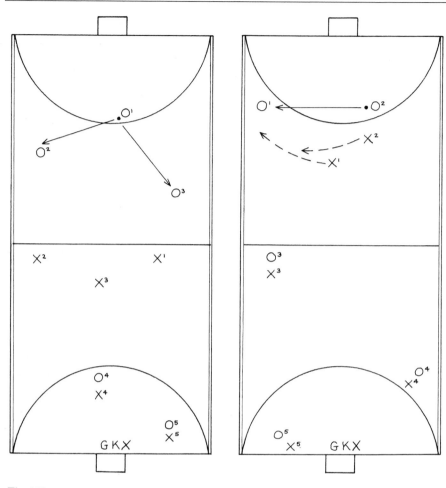

Fig. 113

Fig. 114

understanding on the part of the defending team to counter. This system is best used with experienced players.

In general, a system which employs the strengths of both the man-to-man and zonal systems should be used – the tight man-to-man marking being employed on attackers in the defenders' half, and a semi-zonal system being used on the attacking players in the opposing half.

With this system the forward players X^1 and X^2 work as a pair, with one of them closing down the player on the ball while the other provides the cover to deny the player on the ball room to play the ball forward with a pass or dribble. So, if O^2 has the ball, then X^2 marks him and X^1 provides the cover to the left and slightly behind X^2. If the ball is moved to O^1 then X^1 must move quickly across to mark while X^2 moves to provide the cover to the right and slightly behind X^1. (See fig. 114)

If either O^1 or O^2 makes a run off the ball into the defending half or circle, then either X^1 or X^2 must follow to mark them.

Penalty strokes

A penalty stroke is taken from a spot 7 metres from the goal line. The player taking the stroke is allowed to push, flick or scoop the ball into the goal, and must take no more than one step in executing the stroke.

In theory it should be easy to score a goal from a penalty stroke. In fact, an unusually large number of penalty strokes are missed or saved. It is important, therefore, that players practise this skill regularly and that the coach/teacher makes certain that several players in the team are capable of taking penalty strokes.

Players taking penalty strokes should be advised to decide where they intend to place the ball and to set out to do just that without changing their minds. They should concentrate on the task at hand and not be put off by any delaying tactics or gamesmanship by the opposing goalkeeper.

As every player has their own way of taking penalty strokes the final execution of the shot should be left for the individual to decide. The coach/teacher can of course help by advising about the strengths and weaknesses of the opposing goalkeeper if these are known.

A well taken penalty stroke will invariably lead to a goal, even if the goalkeeper knows where the ball is going. The best areas to shoot at are the four corners of the goal (see fig. 35). It cannot be stressed strongly enough that every team needs a number of players capable of taking penalty strokes, if only because:

1. The best penalty stroke taker might be on the substitutes' bench.

2. The best penalty stroke taker might be injured.

3. The best penalty stroke taker might be having an 'off day' and may have lost confidence in his/her own ability to take the stroke.

4. If the game is drawn it may have to be decided on a barage of penalty strokes, in which case three or even five players from the team will be required to take them.

DEFENDING PENALTY STROKES

As a well taken penalty stroke should result in a goal, the goalkeeper must not gamble on where the ball is going. The goalkeeper should concentrate on the stroke taker, try to pick up as many clues as possible about where the ball is going to be placed and react to the shot. Statistics show that a large proportion of penalty strokes are badly executed and can be saved. If the goalkeeper gambles, he/she may make the occasional spectacular save but will miss many easier and saveable strokes.

During practice sessions targets such as bibs and cones can be put in the goal for players to aim at.

9

Goalkeeping
by Denise Griffiths

Denise Griffiths, *vice-captain and goal-keeper of the England Indoor squad, comes from Lancashire and qualified in Physical Education from the I.M. Marsh College of P.E. in Liverpool. She plays indoor hockey 'because she got bored playing goalkeeper outdoors' – an inspiration for all aspiring goalkeepers reading this knowledgeable chapter!*

The nature of the game of indoor hockey (i.e. the smaller playing area and fewer players on the pitch than in the outdoor game) gives the goalkeeper a higher level of involvement, which makes this position both exciting and fun to play. The strengths and weaknesses of a goalkeeper have a great effect upon the result of the game.

The goalkeeper:

– is often the first line of attack.

– is often the last line of defence.

– must be able to maintain concentration throughout the game.

– must have a sound knowledge of tactics.

– must have a high level of physical fitness, strength, mobility and flexibility to react with speed and confidence while wearing additional equipment.

Equipment

The equipment needed by a goalkeeper is very extensive and can be costly, but it is of vital importance to ensure sufficient protection to reduce injury and boost confidence. Generally, it is best to obtain the best quality equipment, which should be sturdy enough to withstand hard wear and impact and yet light enough to ensure maximum mobility. Some small pieces of padding may be home-made. Kit should include:

1. *Training shoes:* with good 'gripping' soles.

2. *Kickers:* which should provide maximum protection of the foot, while allowing the sole to be in contact with the floor. The wedge-shaped kicker will help to prevent the ball from lifting when kicking.

3. *Leg guards:* should be light and comfortable and offer maximum protection.

4. *Hip and abdomen padding:* this should be sufficient to ensure as much comfort as possible when hitting the floor or stopping a shot. Male players should wear a box protector.

5. *Chest padding, or chest protector:* which should be light and comfortable without restricting movement.

6. *Elbow pads:* these are necessary to prevent skinning and bruising when landing on the floor.

7. *Gloves:* these are essential items of equipment which must be well padded, especially on the left palm and the backs of fingers, but must also enable

An indoor hockey goalkeeper in full kit.

the stick to be held comfortably. The gauntlet variety are preferable as they also offer protection to the lower arm.

8. *Mask or helmet and mask*: this must give maximum vision and be of moulded plastic or of the 'plastic covered-barred' variety.

Goalkeeping is made up basically of two types of style: the goalkeeper who plays on the line and stops anything which comes at any height, and the goalkeeper who moves out and smothers shots as they are taken. Whichever method is chosen depends largely on the individual's strengths and the situation, but generally both methods should be employed during the game. For either method, the goalkeeper must master skills and show a high level of fitness.

Fitness

The padded person should be as fit as any other member of the team, but should also have a great deal of mobility and lightening reflexes. Practise is important since the keeper must expect to spend a fair amount of time diving onto the floor – he/she should be mobile enough to spring back to his/her feet immediately. A goalkeeper should be very fast over 5 metres in full gear and be able to change direction during and after sprints. Goalkeeper's injuries, generally bruises and strains, should be treated as soon as possible and players should not be allowed to shrug them off.

A goalkeeper's reflexes tend naturally to be fast, but they nevertheless need to be improved. One useful and enjoyable practice situation is 'madball'. Three to four players gather in the circle, with about four tennis balls between them. Each tennis ball is hit at the goal and kept going for as long as possible, without it going out of the circle. It may rebound from back and side walls. The goalkeeper attempts to save each ball and clear it out of the circle where it becomes 'dead'. When all four tennis balls have been killed the goalkeeper thoroughly deserves a rest.

Basic goalkeeping skills

KICKING

The ball must remain flat to the floor, therefore it is most important to keep the body weight forward and onto the kicking foot after sending the ball. The goalkeeper should be confident at kicking with either foot and be able to achieve the desired direction, i.e. around the opposition, and to set up an attack. Kicking can be practised well using tennis balls which exaggerate any fault in technique:

1. Using two benches lain sideways and at right angles to one another, the keeper practises kicking the ball with alternate feet onto alternate bench surfaces. The goalkeeper should not stop the ball between kicks, but should attempt to move his/her feet into the correct position. This situation may be pressurised by playing the ball harder against the benches.

2. Six or more balls are placed around the circle. The goalkeeper moves forward and kicks each ball in turn, those on the left side of the circle with the left foot and those on the right with

the right foot. After each ball is played the keeper returns to the goal line facing the ball at all times. Each run may be timed and recorded. The situation may be further pressured by having targets on the side walls to aim for.

ANGLES

The goalkeeper should always assume a position of readiness in the centre of any angle from the ball to the goal. As the ball moves so should the goalkeeper, with a sideways shuffling action, always presenting the face of the pads to the ball.

Angles to the goal should be practised continually during the game, even when the ball is at the other end of the pitch. At these times the goalkeepers should be in a position of readiness, i.e. on their toes, alert and concentrating about half way to the edge of the circle so that they are in a position to challenge a breakaway attacker on the edge of the circle or to retreat to the goal line.

A useful practice is to place about eight players around the edge of the circle, each with one ball. Players, in turn, push the ball at goal and the goalkeeper adjusts his/her position to save each shot. The goalkeeper may be put under pressure by (a) varying the height and pace of the shots, (b) taking the shots from alternate sides, or (c) numbering the players and calling out numbers at random to shoot.

LINE SAVES

Depending upon the height of the shot, the goalkeeper uses a variety of techniques to prevent the ball crossing the goal line. If the ball is low then the goalkeeper would stretch to reach it with a foot and if possible play the ball out with the same action. It is preferable to place both pad and foot behind the ball as opposed to just the foot. This is a difficult skill but can be helped by lifting the knee and driving hard from the back leg to slide the foot and pad across together, so that the body weight finishes on the leading leg.

The goalkeeper must also be prepared at times to dive in order to save the ball with his/her hand or stick, or both, and should ensure a position of readiness before the shot is made. This can be a position whereby the stick is held in two hands and the appropriate hand removed to save the shot while the other remains on the stick. This can be confusing for the inexperienced goalkeeper and sometimes can take longer than holding the stick in the right hand and diving across with both stick and hand together, rather like a goalkeeper in soccer. In the latter method, having the stick and hand together provides a greater surface area with which to save the ball. In either situation the goalkeeper should be encouraged to hit the floor with the hip first, and to spring up instantly and to regain a central position − they should not fall backwards. It is the speed of getting up which is often more important than the speed in getting down!

Line work can be practised with a feeder using tennis balls operating from around the penalty spot. The balls should always be thrown from ground level and the area around the goal should be matted when practising dives. It is often beneficial to practise with the goalkeeper (a) sitting, (b) kneeling, and (c) squatting. The feeder can pressurise the keeper as he/she gains more confidence and ability by feeding the ball faster and to the corners of the goal.

SMOTHERING SHOTS

The goalkeeper should be very quick to smother shots from any unchallenged player in the circle. In a 1 v 1 situation when the attacker is approaching, the goalkeeper should get to the edge of the circle quickly to prevent an early shot. He/she then blocks off the goal by getting as close to the player as possible and placing his/her body on the angle to the goal. The keeper must be prepared to dive to either side if the player attempts to take the ball around him/her and to use the stick on the open- or reverse-side to make as big an obstacle as possible. The goalkeeper should try to 'shepherd' the attacker to the goalkeeper's right side and onto the attacker's reverse stick, thus delaying the shot until the defenders arrive. It is always important that the goalkeeper should keep his/her eyes on the ball and not be tempted to flinch or turn the head away.

These techniques are best practised with the aid of an 'unpadded' player and can be pressurised in a number of ways.

1. The goalkeeper starts on the goal line. Player 1 carries the ball into the circle and shoots. The goalkeeper moves out quickly, smothers the shot on the edge of the circle, gets up at speed and returns to the goal facing the ball. As soon as **GK** returns player 2 repeats the practice from the other side.

The same practice can be used with players 1 and 2 attempting to dribble past the goalkeeper before shooting.

2. The goalkeeper starts the practice by calling, whereupon Player 1 dribbles to gate A and shoots. The goalkeeper must reach cone B and move across to save the shot before retreating to the goal line where a further call will release the next player. This should be practised from the left side so that the goalkeeper has to dive to the left.

STICKWORK

The most important skill in indoor hockey is to maintain possession of the ball and since the goalkeeper is an involved member of the team he/she is often called upon to support his/her team-mates and make passes. The goalkeeper must know when and how to send the ball to a team-mate's stick, how to use the boards, and must know how to tackle on both sides. All these skills should be practised with the other team members and, whenever possible, in full kit.

ORGANISATION OF THE CIRCLE, AND DEFENCE OF FREE PUSHES AND CORNERS

Goalkeepers should have complete control of their defending circle. Their defence should react to their calls (which should be clear and accurate) to mark or move position immediately. At all times goalkeepers should be cool, should maintain control and should not panic themselves or the defenders.

At free pushes goalkeepers must ensure that all danger areas are covered by their defenders or be prepared to cover them when necessary. They should then adopt a low position with their sticks on the floor, ready to intercept a pass or smother a shot. They should attempt to clear the ball to their own players in space and not over their own goal line.

In defending corners, goalkeepers should assess the situation carefully and decide whether they should move off their goal line to block the shot at source or remain on the line and make any saves there. Their decision should be based on:

a knowledge of opponents' corner routines seen in other games.

b knowledge of opponents' corner routines already used against them.

c whichever method they are best at.

Whatever the goalkeeper decides to do he/she must organise his/her defenders accordingly.

It is a tremendous asset to a team if a goalkeeper has the ability to defend successfully a penalty corner, but it must be remembered that against a good corner routine any touch of the ball is a bonus and the goalkeeper should not get too disheartened if a couple of goals are conceded.

Any goalkeeper, at any level, makes mistakes. The nature of the position involves making decisions very quickly and at times the goalkeeper is bound to make the wrong one. Mistakes should be forgotten during the game but afterwards individuals should be encouraged to be critical of themselves and to look for an answer to the problems. Goalkeepers should be helped to be super-confident as they are an invaluable member of a team, both for their performance and their effect on team morale. It often follows that a team with a good goalkeeper is a winning one!

10

Team management and coaching at matches

All players look to matches as the reason for practising, particularly young and inexperienced players who need this 'carrot'. It is therefore most important to try to give as many players as much match practise as possible.

At all levels, careful thought and good organisation before, during and after a match can lead to a more organised, disciplined and successful team.

At school and club level the PE teacher/club captain usually takes on the role of coach and manager. Indeed, at club level, the captain is usually playing as well. The ideal situation would be to have a coach and manager who are non-playing members of the group, and a playing captain. This is obviously not often possible at school and club level, but is a situation which those teams striving to raise their own standard might perhaps like to consider.

We would expect the roles of the manager and coach to be:

Manager

1. Pre-match organisation to include
   - team kit
   - arrangements for the match, travel
   - team numbers
2. (a) At the match
   - spare team kit
   - practice balls
   - first aid kit
   - half-time drinks
   - clarification of rules – particularly at tournaments

(b) During the match
   - sit on the bench
   - organise moving team possessions to the other bench at half-time
   - deal with the mechanics of substitutions – the decisions being made by the coach
   - deal with any slight injuries
   - analyse any particular aspects of the game as requested by the coach
3. After the match
   - ensure all players' and teams' possessions are taken away

A well organised manager will most definitely help players to be more relaxed and mentally prepared for a match.

Coach

The task of the teacher/coach is twofold:
1. to get the best out of each individual player, and
2. to blend the skills of all the individuals in the team into one effective, cohesive unit.

The coach is not just concerned with the teaching/coaching of basic skills, techniques and tactics, but also with developing the correct approach and attitude to the game as well. This can only be acheived by creating an effective coaching/learning situation. If this situation is successfully created then it is generally accepted that players will learn something even without direct coaching.

To coach well one needs to know and understand the game of indoor hockey from a technical and tactical point of view. Without a knowledge or appreciation of the degree of difficulty involved in playing the game a coach cannot expect to begin to do the job effectively.

The greater one's knowledge and understanding of the game, the better one is able to coach. The better one's coaching, the better the players become. The better the players, the better the team becomes. The better the team, the more successful it is likely to be. The more successful the team, the more enjoyment the players are likely to get out of the game.

Important aspects in coaching

Much of this success and enjoyment will be bound up in *what* one coaches and *how* one coaches it.

Coaching indoor hockey, like coaching any other game, has to be structured to be effective. The important ingredients are the ability and motivation of the players and the knowledge and skill/understanding of the coach. To get an effective mix the sessions have to be structured, logical, meaningful and purposeful. Without these ingredients all coaching will cease to have direction. For direction to be established and maintained it is essential for the coach to have:

Aims
These are usually concerned with long term matters, e.g. to improve the team's defensive play. Of course, many factors will affect defensive play − basic skills, individual technique, tactical awareness and, inevitably, fitness. The coach will have to decide which of these factors need to be developed and in what order so that the defensive play of the team can be improved.

As a result a number of short term objectives will emerge.

Objectives
Once the short term objectives have been established, it is up to the coach to determine the order in which they have to be tackled. He/she must decide if it is poor basic skills that are affecting the defensive play, or if it is a lack of fitness which is causing a breakdown in basic skills. Deciding which aspects of the game need to be practised and in what order will depend to a large extent on the coach's observations.

OBSERVATION
There are two levels of observation:
1. *Objective observation* − which is closely related to the coach's ability to think logically and analytically.
2. *Subjective observation* − which is often the emotional reaction of the coach to a situation in which he/she is subconsciously trying to resolve his/her own, rather than the team's, problems.

It goes without saying that to be effective a coach must develop the ability to make objective observations at all times. To be objective a coach must observe:
1. The total performance of all the players in the team and must ask what needs to be done in general terms − is it the technique of the players that needs improving, or is it the tactical awareness of the team that needs developing? Having decided which area he/she needs to work on the coach will need to look for:
2. the specific performance of individual players and must ask if what is required is within the players'

capabilities. The coach must also discover if there are any other factors (fitness, injury or anxiety) which need to be overcome before progress can be made. It is, therefore, important that the coach obtains and analyses all the relevant facts before setting out to improve the performance of individual players and the team as a whole.

ANALYSIS

A coach's opinion will carry much more force and conviction if supported by facts. The analysis of these facts helps in deciding what to coach and how to coach it. It is important for the coach to remember that in any learning situation it is extremely difficult for players to develop several aspects of play at one time. All practices must, therefore, follow a logical sequence with one aspect at a time being improved.

If a coach gets the practices out of sequence they will cease to be meaningful or beneficial. In most cases this happens because the coach assumes skills and techniques in the players which they have not yet acquired. For example, if the defensive play is poor it may be because the players' tackling is weak. It would be important to start improving the tackling on the open-stick side before moving onto reverse-stick tackling. When the coach is satisfied with the development of these skills he/she can introduce practices which concentrate on improving the marking and covering of the team.

PLANNING

It is important, therefore, that coaches devote time and energy to planning coaching sessions in advance. Planning should take into account such matters as:

Facilities – the size of the pitch, the type of surface, floor markings, lighting.

Equipment – the number of goal posts, quality of side-boards, the provision of cones, bibs, balls, sticks, etc.

Personnel – the number of players, their age, experience and ability. The provision of umpires, physiotherapist and the opposition if a pactice match is to be played.

Time – the amount of time available overall. The amount of time to be spent on fitness training, basic skill practices, set piece practice, conditioned games, tactical play and the full game. Even the length of breaks and rest periods should be accounted for in advance. Good planning makes sound organisation possible.

ORGANISATION

Organisation is concerned with the way in which the coach puts his/her plans into action. It is concerned with making sure players know:

a what to practise, and

b how to practise.

What to practise

The players must know which skill, technique or tactic is involved. They should also know the number of players involved, the equipment required, i.e. balls, bibs, cones, etc., and the area of the pitch involved, i.e. the attacking circle, defending circle, the goal, etc.

It is important that practices are realistic and related to the age, ability, experience and fitness of the players concerned, as well as being related to the game.

How to practise

Coaching is concerned with how to practise correctly. This principle must apply whether the practice is related to a basic technique or to an advanced tactical ploy. What is vitally important is that the type and quality of the practice is correct and that each player understands its purpose and his/her function in its organisation.

Coaches who insist on high standards will go a long way to developing good habits and correct attitudes in players. In achieving this a coach can bring about remarkable improvements in individual and team performances.

COMMUNICATION

The ability to observe, analyse, plan and organise will count for nothing if a coach lacks the ability to communicate. Communication can be both visual and oral/vocal.

Visual communication – can be made with the aid of films, diagrams and demonstrations.

Oral/vocal communication – can take the form of commentary or verbal explanation. It is of great help to coaches when clarifying what is being shown or demonstrated. The ability to speak clearly and confidently, like playing, requires practice. This is an area which many knowlegeable coaches have underestimated and ignored at some cost. The advice from those who have been successful is always 'keep it simple and make it clear'.

MOTIVATION

The importance of effective communication in coaching is often demonstrated in the way in which coaches are able to effect remarkable improvements in the performances of players during practices and in games. Much of the time it is not so much what the coach says but how he/she says it which produces the desired results.

Of course, learning and coaching are influenced by many individual psychological factors and the coach's traditional pep talk may be helpful, harmful or largely irrelevant, depending on the individuals involved.

Anxiety, arousability and motivation are all central factors in sporting performance and the coach must take account of these factors and individual needs when trying to motivate players. Some players need to be 'lifted', others 'relaxed'. No coach will motivate a gold medal into a player who simply doesn't want one and despite what has been said about the importance of winning there are still many players, even in competitive sport, who derive as much pleasure from participating as they do from winning. Teaching and coaching can and should be the catalyst for both enjoyment and success.

The demands on a modern coach, even in an amateur game like indoor hockey, are enormous. He/she must combine a sound knowledge and appreciation of the game with an understanding of the psychological factors which affect motivation and learning, all of which must be blended to create an effective coaching situation in which the skills of the players can be moulded into a cohesive, effective and successful unit.

Coaching, like most other skills, improves with practice: it just requires the simple things to be done well.

COACHING IN THE GAME

It is generally accepted that most of a coach's work will have been completed before the match begins, but unlike coaches of many other games, the indoor coach can have a powerful influence during the game through the use of substitutes. A good change or vital instruction at the right moment can decide a match result.

WHEN TO SUBSTITUTE

1. Usually only when the ball has crossed one's own goal line and one's own team has possession of the ball so that the substitution can take place without too much pressure.
2. It is sometimes necessary to substitute when the ball has crossed the oppositions' goal line, if this is the case the substituting obviously *must* be done quickly as the opposition have possession of the ball.
3. After a goal has been scored.

WHY SUBSTITUTE?

1. To rest tired players.
2. To take off a player who is showing poor form – playing badly.
3. To give a player who is upset a chance to cool down.
4. To replace an injured player.
5. To convey instructions to the team while the game is in progress.
6. To break up the oppositions' rhythm if the run of play is going against you.
7. To bring a player with a special ability into the game at a specific moment.
8. To give substitutes court time when the game allows it.

HOW TO SUBSTITUTE

1. Never a whole team at once.
2. Substitute attackers for attackers, and defenders for defenders, unless a player is confident in the role of another court position.
3. Generally, attackers are required to cover more ground and need to work harder than defenders so they need to be substituted more often.
4. Defenders are usually the play-makers of the team and should be kept on the court for as long as possible to give the team a sound base to work from. Only when defenders show signs of fatigue – poor marking, bad tackling and passing – should they be substituted and then only until they are fully recovered – usually 2-3 minutes.
5. Aim to keep the strongest team on the court for as long as possible.
6. Never let the clock dictate when to substitute, i.e. players playing five minutes then automatically being substituted.
7. Always ensure there are players on the court with the ability to perform certain key functions, e.g. short corner strikers, penalty stroke takers, post players for defending corners, etc.
8. It takes time for players to get into the pace of the game and therefore it is unwise to substitute more than two players at any one time, particularly in a closely contested match.
9. The goalkeeper may be replaced by another court player, but this should only happen as a last resort when the team is totally committed to attacking and scoring goals, i.e. if the team must score more goals to win or qualify in a

tournament.

This additional court player must be accustomed to the role, and the team must retain possession of the ball for this tactical substitution to prove effective.

10. During the last few minutes of the match, if the team is winning, it is advisable to have players on the court to keep calm and tight in defence and who are able to concentrate under this pressure.

11. When substituting, ensure the player going on does not step onto the court until the player coming off has stepped off.

12. An individual who has been substituted off should immediately sit next to the coach on the bench, so that the coach can if he/she chooses make relevant comments to the player.

Index